Crowns

By:
Jonathan

Crowns
Book Two of the Series *The Nine*
May 22, 2018, *First Edition*

Copyright © 2018

Cover Photo Credit: Tom Coe

All rights reserved. This book or any portion thereof may not be reproduced or used in any manner whatsoever without the express written permission of the publisher except for the use of brief quotations in a book review or scholarly journal.

ISBN-13: 978-1-942967-30-9

KreativeMinds Publishing
www.kreativeminds.net

Ordering Information:

Special discounts are available on quantity purchases by corporations, associations, educators, and others. For details, contact the publisher at the above listed address or the email address below.

U.S. trade bookstores and wholesalers: Please use the email address below.
email: publishing@kreativeminds.net

To His Wonder, through whom all things are possible.

*Always,
Jonathan*

Introduction

...

It is upon this rock that we stand and proclaim to others all that was and all that will be. It is upon this rock that the waters of the Earth are held — a source of nutrients, a source of life. And as time passes, slowly His plan is revealed in both song and spirit. The words that encase my soul should be seen in such a similar way — as a guidepost and source of hope for others. As a rock houses water, this book — and each book previously and subsequently written — should serve as a source of nutrients, a source of life ever-after. The words are the embodiment of a truth spoken not in action, but in spirit. It is only through His will and mercy that I may ask that these words find resonance within your soul. It is only through His grace that such a beauty can unfold. All my Love, all my passion, all my desire — may it speak to you as it has spoken to me, and may the journey be as grand as you could hope and ever dream it to be.

Always,
Jonathan

...

Prologue

Beginnings.

The art of anything that could ever come into being must first start its days on Earth in the form of potential – vast possibilities of all that could be. From everything that ever was and everything that could one day become, the nothingness that preceded the universe came into being solely through motion and the addition of an observer. When the Spirit of All added a lens to observe a portion of The Great Expanse, the potential of everything became all that could be experienced. Motion set forth a sea of potentialities – where the choice in direction created the experience of an endless array of possibilities and outcomes – each correct in their own rite.

It can be called the "big bang." Or, it can be called "the center of the universe." But in understanding that the placement of an observation point above a portion of All That Is, a lens to view the potential of everything that ever was and everything that ever could be was formed. That lens, by the very nature of the properties of a lens, created perspective and time. For to observe and experience the potential of anything that could be, and not just be all-knowing, meant that God had to set forth the observer into motion – to swing around and through the vastness of everything, however big and however small it may be relative to earthly understanding.

Perspective created linearity and what mankind best understands as time. Though on Earth we observe this linearity in the form of a line, linearity should best be understood as the motion along arcs and curves – all perfect in ratio and proportion. This motion of the observer through the great expanse of All That Is, by its very nature, creates a divide in the heavens. For since an observer was created, it would mean that there is now something that could not be observed in its entirety. And if a lens is understood as one directional, there is always something remaining outside of the periphery left unobserved. This is the very essence of light and darkness, the sun and the moon, above and below, the inside and out. Every opposite must exist when a portion of a substance is divided. For what is darkness, but the absence of light?

And so along that divide and the countless subdivisions of this one concept, galaxies were formed, solar systems were created, stars were born, planets took shape, moons found their homes, and eventually man was birthed upon the Earth – formed from the clay, given life through the breath of All That Is. The rocks on Earth hold the one single nutrient required for life – water. Rocks are the very metaphorical embodiment of the body and spirit, and is the reason why mankind is said to be formed from clay. And through the experience of our walk upon the Earth, we each begin to seek understanding in why we are here, what the purpose in creation holds, and what is hidden within ourselves.

Prologue

Our bodies hold within them the very light of creation, a kingdom within, a light seeking to extinguish darkness. It is the nature of existence. And if the world that we live in – the very understanding of what mankind thinks it knows about everything – is to be seen merely as darkness, then only through finding inner light and helping others find their own light, can darkness find its end. The very action of helping others find their inner light could best be understood through the experience of the emotion, Love. Though Love's popular connotation carries a much different meaning in the traditional earthly walk, Love is a guidepost – the grand denouement and defining moment that helps lead each person Home. Home is not the experience of earthly Love, but rather unity with the Heavens. And while most believe that Love is the fairytale ending, it is really just the beginning of an even greater story to be told for those able to hear and for those able to see.

And so as it was, the conclusion of Gravity Calling left the ending of the Not-So-Cinderella story full of the potential of everything that could be with Lindsey as I stood with my feet in the sand, embracing only the motion of the Spirit inside of me as I journeyed toward the Promised Land. The very North Star that she represented was a light that illuminated the Heavens for me – a light bright enough for me to take notice and feel its gravity calling me home. In the distance upon the horizon, the Promised Land had fallen into view, though it was just a silhouette as the rising sun began to warm my flesh and soul on its upward ascent into the sky. These were the

Crowns

days that would define my Deuteronomy, the fifth chapter of my journey into an epic Love story to unfold – a beginning of a great romance with the Heavens and the Earth – a Love unending, a Love in grace and in kind. This is where this portion of the story begins again.

The Space Between

Starglass.

Shapes of magnificent geometry whimsically falling down in the most perfect crystalized patterns that a man could ever long to see. The light reflecting off of the soft white-colored ground and the white clouds above collide into a montage of glitter and glimmer, sparkling in a majestic rip of lightning throughout all of the fragments of glass raining down from the sky. This is the site I awoke to on February 8, 2014, as the Nashville skies were filled with the first true snowfall of the year – the first hints of God's hands holding His creation during the coldest days of the season. I can only think that a first snow is like seeing the most Loving smile for the first time after a prolonged absence – though it is not that God is truly absent during the winter months. Rather, the winter months make it easy to forget His masterpiece of creation during a time when warmth is absent and the sun is hidden from the eyes. But that first snow…oh, how it warms the soul in such an impossible way, like a smile warms the soul on an emotional, blustery day.

The last several months I have been blessed to experience a journey of the greatest kind. It is the kind of journey that a child could only dream about, a fantasy to the most rational mind. But in the greatest twist of the word, it is the journey that has been a kind greater than Love could ever hope to desire. The journey has poured out a dream onto the canvas of life where I have been caught in the flow of the paint upon the surface while His hand has masterfully pushed around the blobs of colors creating a picture where its true beauty can only be seen from His omniscient point-of-view. To awaken to snow falling down on February 8th was like a celebration of a divine parade with streamers falling from the sky in recognition of reaching the next starting line of the journey.

The journey that I speak of began a little over two years prior to February 8th. It was on the day following Thanksgiving in November of 2011 that I had reached a point of absolute darkness – a darkness that others would not quite see as such, though blackness encumbered the entire field of my vision. It was the day that I finally realized I was not in control of my life and that I never was. A series of seemingly unfortunate situations in both my professional career and personal life led me to a moment of shear desperation, searching for any sense of grounding to the world I once knew. If the prior thirty years of my life could be seen as unfolding to a divine playbook, the period of time between my thirtieth birthday on May 9th leading up to the day after Thanksgiving on November 25, 2011, should be seen as the days that the playbook was cast aside as my Father said, "Son, this may sting a little, but it is necessary so that you can discover all I have in store for you – that is if you are willing to seek Me out."

The Space Between

On November 25, 2011, I prayed and sought help from my Father – asking Him to help show me whatever it was that I was missing…whatever it was that led me into this place of darkness. After my prayer I was led to reach out to my cousin Bryan, who I had not spoken to in several years. Perhaps it was divine timing. Perhaps my call echoed the same feelings that Bryan was experiencing at the same time in his life. Or, perhaps it was always meant to happen this way. Regardless, it was during this call that our conversation on catching up divinely transitioned to a conversation of how we each had a recognition that something was different in our lives – something spiritual. Though we were each faith-driven men, both baptized in our childhoods, there was a call to explore this aspect of our lives further. I brought science to the table in hopes that I could "prove" whatever it was that we spiritually recognized in a way that could help others in the future. And while this was short-lived along the journey, we decided to embark on a spiritual journey together, one where we would practice meditation and deep prayer in an effort to better hear God's voice.

After our phone call, God spoke to me in the boldest of ways – a way I was clearly not expecting. This was the first time I would hear His voice in the darkness and begin to proactively seek Him out in ways that stretch most religious comfort-zones. These were the days that my spiritual eyes began to observe shapes and colors and when my spiritual ears began to hear His voice. This is how this portion of the journey began, though it wasn't until nearly a year into the journey that I really began to gather my bearings and start to understand the meaning of it all.

In the first book of this series – Gravity Calling – I began to see the journey as an epic Love story into the unknown – a story I referenced as a Not-So-Cinderella story due to how much grander the journey was than a Disney fairytale could ever tell during a ninety minute story. Somehow, it seemed that God was leading me home on a chariot of Love guided by the wings of angels. During the first book, the beginning of the journey was unveiled in both scope and destination. A woman named Lindsey, who was divinely placed into my life years prior to these days of discovery, resurfaced in the fall of 2012 causing a flame to rekindle within. About halfway through the book, the story in learning to hear His voice began to find a destination through Love. The first book closes with a proclamation in recognition to His destination as preparations had been made to usher in a symbolic celebration of the Love he was guiding us each toward all along.

The end of Gravity Calling shared the plans of meeting Lindsey in a coffee shop (the next time we would see each other again) where I planned to give her the finished copy of Gravity Calling – a version of the book specifically for her that contained some misleading "filler" chapters at the end so if she attempted to read the end of the book first, she would not see the story that God was penning all along or see how she was the centerpiece used by my Father to help me find Love again. And, by Love, it is important to explain that the Love spoken about is a Love greater than earthly Love. It is a Love of

The Space Between

Heaven and Earth as One; a Love of destiny and happenchance bound by the heartstrings tied by God's hands.

The book was to be given with several other symbolic items that would seem as a fun, innocent gesture to go along with her taking the time to read the book. I planned to not tell her that she was even mentioned in the book, but rather just let her discover it during her own reading after we caught up over times past and parted ways. The final chapter that she would read ends with a letter to her revealing all of the symbols included with the items that were given to her with the book that day – specifically a coffee mug and a bookmark. Housed inside of the clay of a coffee mug that she was given was a key that would open a safety deposit box at a bank near her work. The contents were not disclosed in the letter, only the cliffhanger leaving it up to her to take the next steps that would write the ending to Gravity Calling. This is where the first book ended and where the portion of this story begins – the space between the time Gravity Calling was finished and when she would receive the book at the coffee shop, as the final chapters foreshadowed at the end of Book I.

So in returning from where we once began, I awoke on February 8th to the first real snowfall of the year in Nashville – a heavenly parade of icy streamers falling down. It was the morning following the final details of the book being polished, the cover artwork being completed, and the book entering into its final form which was sent off to the printer for final validation for the first proof copy to be printed and bound. If there was ever a cause for celebration along the journey, this was the day. This was the day I would awake and say, "It is done. Father I've done all that you have asked. It is now and always was in your hands." There would be nothing else to happen in my interactions with Lindsey until after I received the printed copies and set a date for us to meet up again. This was my Father's will and command. Until that day arrived, the objective was simple: make sure the copy of the book Lindsey would receive was printed and bound on February 14, 2014 – an action that was out of my control, though the date was most important for if the Not-So-Cinderella story was going to be the picture of a perfect Love story painted in hues of midnight-red, laced with moonlight among golden threads in the linen of the canvas, it needed to be manifested into its bound form on the day that is the most symbolic to the Love of All.

Womb of the Moon

Every twenty-seven days, a portion of the moon is shining down from above. On the twenty-eighth day, it is eclipsed by the Earth. This is the moon's cycle and it is no coincidence that many other earthly cycles are tied to this same cyclical calendar. The moon controls the water upon the Earth. It is the reason tides rise and fall, why the atmosphere exists at all, and is the reason that life can thrive upon the Earth. If the sun is seen as the source of life, the moon is the nurturing mother to help life thrive. The varying phases of the moon and how it completes a cycle is bound by an archetypal concept as well. The significance of the twenty-seven days of moonglow demonstrates the architecture of the universe, but most importantly the symbolism in completion. The number twenty-seven is the trinity cubed – the Father, the Son, and the Holy Ghost manifest in three dimensions. And though there is much that can be explored as to why this number contains so much significance in the eyes of God, the reason it is brought up here is to demonstrate the importance of its meanings of completion, of unity, of perfection in All.

On February 14, 2014, the moon would be at its peak – a full moon that would illuminate the darkness with its greatest embodiment of romantic light. It cannot be debated that when the light of the moon is cast upon the face of another, that it is the most forgiving light of all – one that causes perfection to appear in the wake of imperfection. It is the reason that moonlight is so symbolic to romance and Love. It Is, so Love Is. If moonlight walks on the beach were absent of moonlight, then they would be just another day walking along the shoreline where the water kisses the sand. But on this day – February 14, 2014, the day that the Earth celebrates Love – the moon would be at its peak brightness. The womb of the moon would open up and pour its complete embodiment of Love upon the Earth in all of its splendor and awe.

The Earth will not see another full moon on Valentine's Day for another nineteen years. But, it will not see another Valentine's Day with a full moon where the numerical significance of the day embodies Divinity for another thirty-eight years. On the day of February 14, 2052, God's mark upon His calendar will appear again, for the date sums to seven ($2 + 1 + 4 + 2 + 0 + 5 + 2 = 16$, which $1 + 6 = 7$). The numerical significance is only matched in greatness by Valentine's Day of 2014, which demonstrates God's fingerprint in the very same way. So in a cosmic sense, Valentine's Day of 2014 represents the greatest demonstration of God's Love to those with eyes to see His Divine. To couples lost in Love, they may only see a hint of greater romance in the air if the clouds so allow. But for me in this recognition, it was important for every step along Love's journey to embody every intentional pigment upon His canvas, the places where His colors of choice gracefully danced in the moonlight. Even the day all of the work was completed and sent to the printer, I would only see in hindsight that it too fell on a similar fingerprint-kind-of-day.

The moment that the entire journey had been leading me toward was this place in the sand; a place where moonlight bathed the surroundings in Love's most romantic light. For me, it was the location where my Leviticus led me to stand as I waited for my Father's direction to enter into the Promised Land. For Lindsey, she would possibly only see a date in the first few pages of the book that would read, "Published February 14, 2014." And, if all of the pieces were to fall together as planned, the last page of the book would contain the date the book was printed, "February 14, 2014."

And so it was in the time between having the first book submitted to the printer and the first day I would receive the proofed copy, I prayed that the print date would fall on this special day of Love's celebration. It was important for the embodiment of every word written to be bound together on the date that the those on Earth celebrate Love – but even more importantly, to embody the significance of the romance of the light of the full moon upon a day that also carried God's fingerprint. To have a published date is merely a decision in text by the author, but to have a date that the words were first brought into printed form stamped on the last page, is a date that only my Father could offer.

Even through all of my prayers, I would not know until the day I received the printed proof of the book, just how it would all unfold when I would flip open the book to the last page that contained the printed date. Every moment leading to that day was wrapped up in His divine plan. I was merely following along to His voice, finding patience and faith that all He intended would one day be. During the days of waiting, I sought to complete the final preparations for all that I had written about in the book. At the time of writing, I did not have any idea how I would be able to have a key inserted into a coffee mug made of clay. I was unsure of a starting place in seeking out a bookmark that could have a piece of poetry stitched within a false back. And lastly, everything that my Father had shared with me to include inside of the safety deposit box was still just an idea, and had to be brought into existence.

So in all that remained ahead, these were the days of preparation as I awaited the receipt of the book. Lindsey would not know that any of these efforts were taking place. At best, she would only realize there was an absence in our communication. The absence in communication was perhaps the hardest part of it all. For as my Father tasked me with placing my trust in Him alone and removing myself from the equation, my earthly mind wrestled with the idea of how perceived inaction during courting could cause any potential in a future relationship to stall. It was a concept that I would only see in hindsight how truly small the earthly mind is, for Love is a bond that defies action and inaction; it is the trust in our Father; a precision in grand spectacle that transcends time and space, drawing two souls together across impossible bounds. So, as I waited to be her everything, it was only the trust in my Father that remained as she went about her life oblivious to all that was taking place and all that remained ahead.

Bookmark of the Soul

Few expressions can describe how perfect of a moment it is when the written words from one soul are read through the spiritual eyes of another. Perhaps few will recognize it as such, but this spiritual feeling can best be understood when a person reads a book that causes the emotions to unravel in various ways. Maybe this book causes a person to react in sadness, in opposition. Or maybe, it causes the soul to erupt in tears. Merely words from another have the potential to touch the depths of the soul of any reader. It almost defies any rationale how merely words on a page can carry this great of a potential.

Think about the situation of witnessing two people hopelessly, helplessly falling in Love to earthly eyes. There is no doubt that the situation would be polarizing to witness. Some would well up inside with empathic emotions to all that was witnessed. Others may become disgusted as the mind's self-defense system is called into action and attempts to stifle and prevent mere thoughts of happiness from causing any hurt within. It is the most polarizing of all events to witness in earthly sight, but to read it…oh, to read it. The words cause everything to come to life as they touch a part of the soul the human mind's self-defense system cannot protect.

Crowns

Even in the context of a personal Love story, to experience it can be an exhilarating ride, but to read about it and reminisce is untouchable from the experience itself. Often, details are overlooked in the experience that cannot be re-read and understood with the depth and clarity of a written words. Words capture everything the Master-writer intends through the eyes of the earthly experience. How many times can words be re-read and new meanings found? The divide is so great that it creates a chasm impossible to bridge from the experience itself, for only one opportunity is given to process all of the details in the brevity of an experience. When words are written, it is not the mind of the writer pouring out his soul, but rather the writer is serving merely as a vessel for the soul to pour out the words of the Spirit through his hand. We are all souls trapped in bodies, rather than bodies with souls. When this simple context is understood, it is easy to see that words originate from beyond the embodiment of the earthly vessel. They originate in unity, in perfection, in hope, in faith. They originate in the beginning, for they were formed before all else. And all that was formed from the words, is the Word, for it Always Was and Always Is.

The soul is a conduit between the Word and the experience of life itself. Words written from an unobstructed vessel contain the light within. To those who read written words, the light that is invisible to the eye warms the soul within causing it to react in kind. Tears that are formed in recognition of reading written words should be seen as a spiritual recognition of purity and light – words that embody the soul of another's essence and understanding of light. Even the most obstructed vessel receives inspiration of words in the origin in light. Whether the most obstructed vessels color the words written with darkness or allow the light to shine through unimpeded, is another subject entirely. But the point is that all words originate in Love and light. Truth is to be found in all art, in life, in every soulfully written word, and all of the words claimed to be written by the mind. It is only the purity of the vessel that colors the words written, from their point of origin to their point of manifestation.

As I came to understand the importance of how my Father was using my vessel as a conduit for His intentions, I came to understand that Gravity Calling was much greater than just a Love Story – it was His Story painted in Love that I was blessed to experience. While it was important that the words were bound and printed on the fourteenth of February, it was important that every word written carry the purest intention possible, and house layers of meaning that could be studied and understood for generations to come. When the book began, I did not necessarily understand the reasoning I was tasked to do certain things. I was not sure why I was led to put a poem in a bookmark or a key within the clay of a coffee mug. But that is just the way He leads. If I already knew His intentions, there would not be much of a journey. The journey is about learning to see how He works, how He leads, how to follow blindly on faith alone, and how to trust that He will catch you when you fall.

Crowns

As I understood the blind directives, I was still tasked with bringing the directives into existence. The words of Gravity Calling told of a bookmark that housed a poem that would be given to Lindsey when she read the book. As it would turn out, the quest to make this happen turned out to be an exceedingly difficult task in and of itself. My original intention was to find a bookmark with one her favorite Bible verses on it. As a fallback, I would have a custom bookmark made. Though it may seem simple in task, the journey on this portion of the story was one of the most testing upon my soul. To make sure that everything was presented with perfect polish, the bookmark was perhaps the most difficult since it also had to appear as the most unassuming. It could not appear cheap, nor expensive. It could not appear custom made, or poorly made. The alterations to the bookmark to house the poem could not appear out of place, or give rise to the thought of something being "off." Sometimes the greatest challenge a person can ever be tasked to perform, is to make something appear simple, when it is the embodiment of a complexity beyond all norm.

My quest to find the appropriate bookmark led me to every store in the greater Nashville area that could possibly sell bookmarks. It led me to scouring the internet in hopes of finding just one of her favorite Bible verses printed on the front. This was one of the most difficult tasks imaginable. While here favorite verses were found on paper and cardboard bookmarks, it was nearly impossible to find one that was made of any type of cloth or leather material. My search eventually led me to distributors and whole-sellers of bookmarks that required quantity orders. Any custom print jobs (my fall back plan) required large quantity orders as well. As it turned out, having a bookmark made for my requirements was not a simple task. Over days of searching and travelling to every vendor in Nashville, I exhausted all options. The evening I was about to give up on the idea (even though I already had sent the book to the printer), I happened over a website that sold old, out-of-print bookmarks. It was a sign. The company offered two of the verses I sought on faux-leather bookmarks, which appeared to be perfect for the addition of a cloth backside I planned to add to hide the poem. I ordered two of each version of the bookmarks. Forty-five dollars and a couple of days later, I received the bookmarks.

After receiving the bookmarks, it was apparent that only one of the two that would work for my intentions was the bookmark that included the verse 29:11 from Jeremiah. In and of itself, the verse is spectacular in the context of all that it was intended to carry in meaning. On the surface, the words Lindsey would see comprised the verse that she had mentioned was one of her favorites recently, but inside there was much more to be revealed.

...

"For I know the plans I have for you," declares the Lord, "plans to prosper you and not to harm you, plans to give you hope and a future."
- Jeremiah 29:11

...

Crowns

It was important that the bookmark appeared discreet and untouched from the way it would be purchased from a store. Finding a way to modify the back to make it easily accessible while also appearing manufactured was the next challenge. Out of all unlikely places, I eventually asked my tailor who/where she would recommend for such a task. She became excited once she heard the story of the bookmark and wanted to help me out. I obliged, though I was unsure how it would turn out. My tailor showed me how she would unstitch all of the original manufactured stitching and place a cloth backing on the bookmark. We chose an appropriate fabric and I left her with both bookmarks, two copies of the poems, and the faith that she could help make the bookmarks appear untouched from a purchased form.

With great happiness, I received the bookmarks in beautiful form. One bookmark was an example of perfection, while the other had a few minor flaws that would still be undetectable from an unsuspecting recipient. The imperfections were caused from my tailor figuring out the best way to approach the backside stitching. Most certainly, I am thankful for having the foresight to purchase two bookmarks which gave my tailor the opportunity to achieve perfection. After paying my tailor, I could only chuckle in how Lindsey was going to receive the most expensive (yet meant to appear inexpensive and more of an afterthought) bookmark possible. All in all, with shipping, stitching, and in final form, it cost over a hundred dollars to achieve the look required, though money was never a variable in the execution of the task, for my Father had provided the resources to follow His directive.

The words printed on the bookmark could not have carried a better message to accompany the book. If at anytime Lindsey was to look down at the bookmark while reading, she would see a constant reminder that God is preparing the way for her heart. All she had to do was trust in Him. And just as the bookmark carried such a grand message on its surface, the words of Gravity Calling were to be read in a similar manner. It was important for Lindsey to have a bookmark that carried a much greater symbolic meaning that paralleled His story as she read her story that unfolded to a greater message in the end. With each page that would be read, it would be as if she was leafing through the pages of my life, beginning to see the world as I saw it, beginning to see herself through my eyes, beginning to understand a divine Love greater than could be seen through earthly eyes. When the time would arise when she needed to mark her place in the book, it was important that the bookmark contain the embodiment of my soul hidden within its seams. This bookmark of the soul was symbolic of a divine marker placed along the journey – a resting point to catch a breath of spiritual air. The embodiment of the words hidden within would never change over the duration of the journey. The exterior of the bookmark would always appear the same. The poem held within its seams would remain unchanged. It was a marker of what always was and what will always be, bound by thread hidden from her eyes to see.

Crowns

It would only be in the final pages of Gravity Calling that the words would reveal that the bookmark used to mark her stops along the way held a poem within – a poem which described the very first time I met her. Though our first meeting is written about in the pages of Gravity Calling, it is the concise embodiment of the words of the poem that sum up the moment in perfection. The words were not included in the first book, for they were always intended for Lindsey to find within the bookmark when she reached the end of the book. But for now, it is appropriate to include the words here:

...

Fell Into Mine

She spoke not in words, but in spirit
And though the words may have echoed from her lips
I was enchanted by a conversation silent
A silence so profound that my soul responded helplessly in kind
In ache – with a tremble, a tremor, a wake;
I have to believe it registered at the outermost edges of the heavens
An epicenter that all began when her eyes fell into mine.

Always,
Jonathan

The Potter & the Clay

Biblically speaking, there are at least thirty-two references to "clay" in both the Old and New Testaments in the modern Biblical canon. There are at least thirteen references to the word "potter." Though I was caught up in the rollercoaster journey of chasing Love with Lindsey, I failed to catch the significance of this reference in the actions I was called to take in providing her with a coffee mug handmade of clay on the day we would meet for coffee. Sometimes I think I must miss the most obvious signs from my Father but somehow manage to pick up on many of the smaller, supporting details. It is a conundrum that I would not have any other way. For, if I were to only see the obvious, then the details that paint the picture to this story – and the details spilled forth throughout all nine books that define His Story – would be missed in helping tell the tale that is intended to be shared.

Most people catch the headlines in the earthly walk. Few care to explore the inner-workings of how the headlines came to be. But the inner-workings are the most important aspect of the spiritual journey – for the headlines God delivers are the most easily dismissed. Without learning to process the details in how God communicates, the wondrous demonstration of God's Voice falls upon deaf ears. And so is my dilemma in learning to hear His Voice. Often I miss the beach in lieu of scrutinizing over each grain of sand along the journey. It is a difficult balance to find. But without learning how to scrutinize His wonder along the journey, I would never be able to see how I was standing upon a beach in hindsight.

The second item Lindsey was to receive with the book on the day we would meet at an unassuming coffee shop in Nashville was a coffee mug – handmade with a key housed within. The rationale in giving her both the coffee mug and the bookmark was only to subtly hide additional items she would need to continue experiencing the story after the words in the book ended in a cliffhanger revealing all that was hidden. Even after writing the previous sentence, I have to chuckle at how focused I was on the destination without understanding the true intention in God's plan. I understood that the book was to end in a cliffhanger where the ending would be based upon the next steps she took. I also understood that if the book was received as overwhelming in content and story (as I understood would be the likely reception due to the subject matter), then it would have to be interactive with instructions in how to take the next steps.

Looking back, it is kind of funny to think how my Father led me to these concepts while I missed the bigger story in action. For if the book was written as a statement regardless of how open she was to receiving, then it might as well be just another billboard along the roadside. But words should be seen as motion, where the words call to action the soul of another to move. Unbridled words should serve as a guidepost in becoming for the author while helping readers learn to become. And so in this concept, the greatest divine truths of written history can be revealed. For if written words do not serve as motion to the soul where a transparent call to Love is evoked, then the words have been colored by the ego and manipulated by the man in rose-colored glasses.

And perhaps I even missed this analogy in Gravity Calling as to why Lucifer began appearing to me wearing flashy clothes and rose-colored glasses. I never quite put two and two together until this writing as to why the lenses that filtered the light passing into his eyes would tint the world around him in hues viewed as warm and inviting in earthly rationale. In an earthly sense, the phrase "to see the world through rose-colored glasses" is not a negative phrase. Rather, it indicates a person only sees Love and warmth while missing the negative aspects of the world. But perhaps it should best be understood to mean, "to view the world in a way that is favorable to the mind." For, if words are viewed with a favorable distortion to the author, then the purity in the light of the Lord has been tinted in hues of the vessel. As to the man in rose-colored glasses, it makes perfect sense why he would appear in a way that colored his vision to the world in order please his ego. The coloration is an allure to distractors that placate a journeyman along The Way.

So if words are to be written as uncolored, and unbiased as best as a vessel can serve as a light of the soul, it was important that Gravity Calling ended in the manner it did. To Lindsey, she would have received the coffee mug in a simple gesture in our meeting at a coffee shop. It would be easy enough to hand her the book with a bookmark inside of it with no explanation required why a bookmark was placed in the book (her favorite verse would be an added touch). But for her to take the next steps forward, it was important that she receive something that would unlock the next portion of the journey. In older times, it could have been a buried treasure where X marks the spot upon a map or even some form of a scavenger hunt. But, in modern times, locks and keys are the updated version of this concept. In spiritual terms, the symbolism of a lock and key is unrivaled in strength and archetypal meaning.

To Lindsey, she needed to receive a key which unlocked a box filled with everything required for the next steps of the journey. One object. One task. One directive. If she so chose to explore the journey of Love prepared for her, it was a simple task at hand – one which was revealed in the final chapter of Gravity Calling. But to hand her a key directly would be the same as telling her what to do – something that breaks the concept of freewill. The key needed to be hidden within her grasp, later revealed its location, and even revealed what it would unlock. The only way I could figure out how to give her a key was within something unassuming, yet held together with the idea of the book. Bookmarks are flimsy and therefore could not hold a key. The only idea I could arrive at was a coffee cup, though it would have to be custom made.

As it would turn out the process of finding someone who would take the time to hand-make a coffee mug of clay was an

The Potter & the Clay

almost impossible task. I again ran into the problem of having a company manufacture high-quantity orders or finding a local potter who would want to take the time to make a coffee mug by hand. I came to learn that including a key within a handmade clay mug is not a simple endeavor. The kiln used to dry the clay after it has been shaped rises to a temperature hot enough to melt anything made of metal. This meant that the coffee mug could not be made in one piece even though it needed to appear as one solid mug.

After being turned down by the first several potters I spoke with, I eventually was led to a local Nashville potter eager to take on such a challenge. To make it worthwhile to him, I offered to commission two coffee mugs that were identical – one that contained the key in some form of a false bottom baked together with the upper piece, and one that was just a replica of the mug without the key. Again, this was not an inexpensive project for an end product that needed to be simple and not appear handcrafted.

The task was simple, but the process was to take much longer than expected. To create any object out of clay, bake it, paint it, glaze it, and finish it to appear manufactured, was at least a two-week process assuming the potter's first attempts in executing his plan for the two-piece mug worked out flawlessly. This mug would turn out to be another expensive endeavor in creating a simple looking object. But if I was to pass off the gesture in giving her the coffee mug as nonchalant and unassuming with a comment like "my daughter saw it at the store and wanted to get it for you since we were meeting at a coffee shop" or "...and since you will be reading the book, I thought you might as well have a new coffee mug to help you get through the late night reading sessions," the mug required the same care in the craft of its creation.

I have to believe that God must see our earthly world in the same way as He prepared me to see it through the actions with Lindsey. The Bible is the shining example of this very same craft. It is a book of collected writings from those who understood how to hear the Voice of God. Every word written serves as a guidepost for those who will one day seek Him in the darkness. As my journey began to unfold metaphorically to the first five books of the Bible (the Torah), my Father used the journey I was on to help me see how the Bible is a living example of the walk upon the Earth. It contains stories of truth, rule, and law, but it is also the Words of God bound in a way that sets a soul into motion. The words of the Bible serve as a catalyst to the soul, written by vessels that helped His words be communicated in their purest forms.

Though I would not see the reasoning when I was tasked to provide Lindsey with a key housed within the clay of a mug, the concept should be seen as no different than the instructions the Lord provides with the Bible. While there are the Ten Commandments – the laws that define how to sanctify Love upon the Earth – the remainder of the Bible is our Father's artful approach to telling the greatest Love story ever told. Through all of the imperfections of the people upon the Earth, He instills hope in a Love that awaits. He goes insofar as to explain precisely how there is a key housed within the clay of

The Potter & the Clay

each and every person upon the Earth. Throughout the nearly eight-hundred-thousand words in the Bible, the Lord shares example after example of how each person can find this key within the clay of his body and even where it is located. He goes on to reveal there is a locked box that the key will open, and even where that locked box is located. He does not go beyond the revealing of the Kingdom that awaits each person who finds the key and blindly follows His lead, for it is up to each person to discover all that He has prepared for him.

To some, this description may sound as simple as the concept of baptism and opening the heart to allow God in. But perhaps that may best be seen as merely the location of the key. Some may be content in just knowing the key is there. But to be able to use the key, the clay of the body must be broken and shattered across the ground. Only then is the key capable of being used. He has provided instructions on where to find this key as well as where to go to find the lock. From that point forward, it is up to the person to follow the journey and open the box. It is an extremely simple concept that must be the rarest achievement across mankind, for those who have achieved this task are the spiritual elders whose stories have been told throughout the ages.

And while I never saw the task of including the key within the clay as metaphorical to how my Father must see His efforts in guiding people Home, it would begin to be revealed to me in the days leading up to the day I would bare my soul to Lindsey through the words in Gravity Calling. It was only upon this understanding that I began to seek out references to

Crowns

"potters" and "clay" in the Bible. Though I discovered at least thirty-two references to clay, the one that immediately stood out among the others, was a section from The Book of Jeremiah – the same location as the verse that was printed upon Lindsey's bookmark.

...

18:1 This is the word that came to Jeremiah from the Lord: 2 "Go down to the potter's house, and there I will give you my message." 3 So I went down to the potter's house, and I saw him working at the wheel. 4 But the pot he was shaping from the clay was marred in his hands; so the potter formed it into another pot, shaping it as seemed best to him.

5 Then the word of the Lord came to me. 6 He said, "Can I not do with you, Israel, as this potter does?" declares the Lord. "Like clay in the hand of the potter, so are you in my hand, Israel. 7 If at any time I announce that a nation or kingdom is to be uprooted, torn down and destroyed, 8 and if that nation I warned repents of its evil, then I will relent and not inflict on it the disaster I had planned. 9 And if at another time I announce that a nation or kingdom is to be built up and planted, 10 and if it does evil in my sight and does not obey me, then I will reconsider the good I had intended to do for it.

11 "Now therefore say to the people of Judah and those living in Jerusalem, 'This is what the Lord says: Look! I am preparing a disaster for you and devising a plan against you. So turn from your evil ways, each one of you, and reform your ways and your actions.' 12 But they will reply, 'It's no use. We will continue with our own plans; we will all follow the stubbornness of our evil hearts.'"

-Jeremiah 18:1-12

...

The Potter & the Clay

The section in Jeremiah reveals how the Lord uses the example of the potter and the clay to illustrate how He delivers His will upon the Earth. It is a section that parallels greatly to the efforts I was tasked to perform through the demonstration of seeking out a potter to create the clay mug that housed the key for Lindsey. But after reading this verse, another verse referenced in Isaiah began to stand out to me. Isaiah 29:16 reads:

...

You turn things upside down, as if the potter were thought to be like the clay! Shall what is formed say to the one who formed it, "You did not make me"? Can the pot say to the potter, "You know nothing"?
-Isaiah 29:16

...

The verse and chapter numbers were what caught my attention first. As I had just understood how the verse on Lindsey's bookmark originated from the same book of the Bible that contained such a detailed section about the potter and the clay (the Book of Jeremiah), it was apparent that Isaiah 29:16 was another reference to the potter and the clay and it was almost the same chapter and verse numbers as the verse on Lindsey's bookmark. To some, they may say, "almost is not the same as exact." But, it is understanding how the threads woven by God's hand all interconnect where the beauty is revealed. For when I looked up Isaiah 29:11 – the same verse and chapter number as Lindsey's verse from Jeremiah – I could only smile.

Crowns

...

For you this whole vision is nothing but words sealed in a scroll. And if you give the scroll to someone who can read, and say, "Read this, please," they will answer, "I can't. It is sealed."
-Isaiah 29:11

...

The words from Isaiah 29:11 arrived full circle to the poem hidden within the bookmark. If at first the reference to Jeremiah being in the same book as one of Lindsey's favorite verses seemed like coincidence, the thread that was woven between Isaiah and Jeremiah should be enough to remove all doubt in any coincidences while blindly following my Father's lead. But something else unexpected happened in the wake of the efforts to craft the coffee mug. During the weeks I had to wait on the bookmark and mug being completed, God unveiled how all of the next steps were to unfold. Up to this point, I was still blindly following His lead only knowing that the book needed to be completed. And while the book ended in a cliffhanger for Lindsey, I was also left with a cliffhanger in further directives. It was only after the book had been completed, sent to the printer and I had begun to follow the directives of bringing the written words of the coffee mug and the bookmark into existence, that my Father helped me to understand the next steps and how the items in the safety deposit box should also include the replacements for the objects Lindsey would have to break in discovering the poem and the key. There were other items to be included in the box as well, but since the ending of the book required her to break the coffee mug into a million pieces in order to reveal the key and to slice open the bookmark to reveal the poem, it was important to unveil a perfect version of each of the items inside the box the key unlocked. But this was just the beginning of the story of the importance of the box and the contents inside.

Ponte Vedra

On February 25, 2014, I awoke from another amazing experience in the heavens. While I have come to understand that these experiences are becoming more powerful and more regular, each experience still leaves me breathless. After having received the printed proof copy of the book a few days prior and having received the bookmarks stitched with the false backings from my tailor, I was left only to wait for the finishing coffee mugs to be finished. Though I had been undoubtedly anxious during the days surrounding these events, the experience in the heavens provided peace and calm as I pushed through the space between the last time I spoke with Lindsey and the feelings of anxiety foreshadowing our eventual meeting.

It was in this heavenly experience that I received confirmation from my Father that the effort I was taking in bringing the book's final chapters into earthly existence was suitable in His sight. At this point I was still trying to understand the full picture that He was painting in this Love story, but I understood that every step I was led to take was unveiling a little piece of His painting in hindsight. It was on the morning of February 25th, that I was taken to the heavens and placed before one of the beautiful blonde female angels that I see regularly. But this time was different. This time, she wanted me to meet "the potter." I was not sure who the angel was intended to represent – or if perhaps his appearance was only archetypal in form – but she introduced me to the potter and together they celebrated in the efforts I had made in hiding a key within a coffee mug for Lindsey. Though at this point in my journals, the entries were not as detailed as they would one day become, the following is an excerpt from a this portion of my experiences in the heavens on February 25th, 2014:

...

I returned to the heavens to see a blonde angel with a potter. The angel was celebrating my effort of including a key within the clay mug that I planned to give Lindsey. Both the angel and the potter were very proud in the symbolism I was led to use in my efforts with Lindsey.

...

When I returned to my body, I was overcome with joy. To know that the efforts taken on Earth were to be celebrated as they were noticed by the angels is nothing short of endless awe. It would not be until after I received the finished mugs from the potter that I would take all of the contents to the bank to place inside of the safety deposit box. And though it has not yet been revealed all that the box was to contain, it is important to understand that the contents to be included were in motion during this time just as much as the journey I had embarked upon. During these days, my Father began to share with me His plan. Again, I would not understand the symbolism until much later down the line, but I followed His will all the same. It was during this time that I understood that the

Ponte Vedra

contents of the box must be one half of the story for Lindsey, while I completed the other half along my journey.

In the recent months, my Father had begun tasking me with traveling to Florida. I understood there was a strong possibility that moving was His complete intention though I did not have a job that would allow for the move, nor did I have the flexibility in my work schedule for an extended vacation. I really did not have any idea where I was supposed to possibly move to in Florida other than acknowledging His directive to travel to that part of the United States. It seemed like such a strong contradiction to the Love story I was experiencing, for I could not understand why I would be called to move to Florida when it seemed like the Promised Land was the destination of Love in Nashville. But as I sought further guidance, He began sharing with me specific places in Florida that I was to find. I even flashed-back to one of the first conversations with Lindsey where she had responded to a comment I made about moving to Florida about wishing she could just pick-up and move there as well. It had also come up in conversation how her children Love to visit Florida because their dad lives there as well.

In searching for one of the locations I was shown, I discovered it was in Ponte Vedra – a city just south of St. Augustine. But, it was only when I had spoken with my daughter on a phone call that I began to see how God was aligning all of the variables for the fairytale Love story to become a reality. It was in that conversation that I learned that my ex-wife had been dating a man in Jacksonville, Florida, for at least the last six months. The single greatest question I had with the directive to move to Florida was how would I see my daughter as much as I do now. But it was in this moment I started to see how every variable was lined up for a divine play to be called from God's line-of-scrimmage. If everything continued on its course (without knowing anything about a job opportunity), it seemed like my ex-wife would be traveling more frequently to Jacksonville (or even moving to Jacksonville), which would allow me to see my daughter more.

Then there was the fact that Lindsey's ex-husband lived in Florida. And while I did not expect us to somehow up and move on a whim to Florida together, I understood that if I moved to Florida and we were in the beginning stages of dating, it would provide her children an opportunity to see their father more as well. Additionally, the Ponte Vedra location would bring both my daughter and me closer in location to my parents and sister who lived in south Georgia. All in all, it would be a glorious play if God chose to make the call from the sideline. And despite not having any idea how moving to Florida would possibly happen financially for me, I also knew that Lindsey had expressed her desire to move to Florida, but was limited by her job as well. So when it came to understanding the task to explore moving to Florida, I understood it was also intended to carry a symbolic meaning to the Love story being written.

On a day at the very end of February – just after a meeting with one of the potential employers who had left a message on my voicemail when I returned from Haiti (as written about

Ponte Vedra

in Gravity Calling) – I travelled down to Ponte Vedra, Florida to a location that resembled the place I was shown by God. There was a resort I happened across that made for a picture-perfect setting for the next portion of the Love story to be written. Though I did not know if that was even part of His intention on this adventure, I prayed and sought guidance for the next steps I was to take. Even if this location was to be part of His plan, the resort cost more than I could afford. And while it felt like I was divinely led to this location, I had more questions than answers. I still was not sure if the trip to Florida was to seek out ideas for the next portion of the story with Lindsey or if it was intended for me to explore following my Father's lead in moving to Florida. Regardless, I spent the weekend looking at houses, boats, and resorts. I inquired about booking the most magnificent weekend possible for a surprise, romantic weekend getaway, though it seemed too fantastical to be real. Nothing made sense, but it was fun to imagine.

Fitzgerald's World

I am not sure what drives some people to read the last pages (or even last chapter) of a book first, but it has never been the way I have chosen to read a book. To me, I want to see the story told in the way it is intended to be told with all of the twists, turns, and bumps in the road. For if the ending is known before the story has begun, the journey would not hold as much value or incentive to embark upon. Imagine seeing a character's hidden identity revealed in the final pages, or perhaps reading about the twist hidden in all of the pages. Imagine seeing the revelation of the story's journey condensed down into a simple action or sentence of summation. Would that not leave the journey empty?

Though I cannot understand why someone would attempt to read the last page of a story first, it happens nonetheless. It was an inevitable possibility I had to prevent from happening with Lindsey. But to tell someone not to read the last page first is basically saying, "Here. This page is important. I am telling you not to look, but I know you will look anyway." To prevent this possibility, I had to fill the back of the version of Lindsey's book with enough content to keep her guessing. I recognized that even if she flipped to the last page, she may thumb back a few pages prior. I decided to include two chapters worth of misdirection and a "notes" section at the very end. Over the final two chapters of Lindsey's version of Gravity Calling, she would find the words to chapter seven of The Great Gatsby.

It was a chapter that my Father led me to include for symbolic reasons I was not aware of at the time. Since I was also unsure if Lindsey would recognize the dialogue happening in this chapter, I made sure to change the name of the most recognizable character, Gatsby, to another name from Fitzgerald's world. When F. Scott Fitzgerald first wrote The Great Gatsby, the name of the book was titled Trimalchio – a name I would only discover during research. There was not much of a reason I chose to replace the name of the lead character to the name Fitzgerald originally intended other than it was a name I assumed would not be recognized. But as it would turn out, there is always a reason in His grand plan.

Perhaps this is the way that God, our Father must approach each story He is telling, for what would the incentive be to those who already know the ending? Since His Story is about every person's opportunity for salvation through Christ, would it not mean that some people would just expect to reap the rewards of the ending without the journey? Perhaps that is one of the reasons the fervor meant to be experienced in the walk of faith is a walk of empty hearts ignorant to His grace. So much time has been focused on the ending rather than helping others see that it is really about the journey – the definition of faith.

That very last statement is sure to ignite more than a few hearts that will say, "But we do preach and live by the gospel.

Fitzgerald's World

We adhere to it and try to make it living every day. We have faith and believe in Jesus Christ. Through these efforts we have the promise of salvation – the promise of Heaven. We are living each day so that we may see the Kingdom." And, they are not wrong. However, the response may best be understood as a person having read the final page of the Book He has written over thousands of years, expecting to reap the rewards by works alone. Belief and faith embody more than words and thought. Belief and faith are the very demonstration of bringing the fabled journey to life for others to see. It is the motion of a thought manifested into light. For how would our Father ever tell a story that must be experienced in a way unique to everyone? The short answer is He would not. Those who have experienced the journey would. And how would they tell the story? The short answer is they would not. He would. For it can be seen that those who have followed the walk of faith upon the journey's road, would be called to write and called to bring light into the world in ways others could see – to tell the story as they learned to see through the opening of their spiritual eyes when they were found face-to-face, staring into the eyes of our Loving God. The words and the works created, from having the faith to follow His lead, would craft a story to be told throughout the ages, but only tantamount to the last page of a written story.

To some, these words will be tough to stomach. Many will turn to the thought, "But the Bible says…" Again, they are not wrong. Of course the Bible says whatever example would follow that statement, for it embodies the very demonstration of the followers of God (in the Old Testament), and the followers of God through Christ (in the New Testament). Other works demonstrate this very same ideal which often causes divides in religions across the world – followers of God through their written words that others see as The Way. However, some journeys are just more colored in earthly hues than others, marring the perfect words of His Story, which can cause missteps to those imperceptive to the tinted light. But it is important to see how all eight-hundred-thousand-plus words from the English translation of the Bible are a culmination of stories, told through each author's perspective of learning to see our Father's eyes, and in turn, learning to see through our Father's eyes. The Bible is not written by one author, but it Is – a summation of last pages of each author's books, summing into the last page of His.

Often when a person thinks about the works of those people written about in the Bible, it is envisioned in a way that removes earthly perspective. And while it is important to see the words from this perspective, it is also equally important to see these people through the perspective as if they were a friend, a family member, a relative, or a friend of another. For how would these people be received in the presence of the public eye? Most importantly, how would these people be received by your eye? What would convince you that the strength of God is present in him? What would cause you to remove all doubt? Perhaps there is not one solid answer, for every person is on a different part of his journey in learning how to see through spiritual eyes. But, in whatever way a per-

Fitzgerald's World

son would scrutinize another person regarding this question, it would most likely embody doubt. And, with time running out, what would truly make a person say, "I believe?" It is a question that really focuses on a greater question: How would you know you were in the presence of His Grace?

Some may hide behind the false thoughts of, "I will just know" or "because I will." But that type of response is no different than a parent saying, "Because I said so," with no justification. For how can a person see without opening his spiritual eyes? Think of the story of Moses or of Noah. These are people who lived hundreds of years with the stories of their lives summed up in a few hundred words, where only a handful of miracles were performed throughout hundreds of years. And though it should only take one miracle to help others see, people still choose to doubt God. Even the teachings of Jesus were dismissed by most – his disciples included (during his crucifixion). To this day, his teachings are still debated (if not dismissed entirely) by other religions. And to put the New Testament into a different perspective, the majority of the words in the Bible about Jesus were written by a non-believer who had to be miraculously shown The Way after his resurrection. With all of this said – and let it be known that I believe in Jesus Christ – it begs the question, "How would you know?" in modern times. What would you have to see to believe? But perhaps an even stronger question is "why?" What drives the doubt, and what would it take to see beyond the veil?

This latter question is perhaps the best explanation in describing all that is missed from only reading the last page. For those who have not embarked upon the journey, but have read the last page thinking they understand the story – and even live out the story – are the very ones who would not have an answer to "why" or "how" beyond "I will just know" and "because I will." These are the ones who are possibly the most lost along the way – a dismantling state of affairs upon the spiritual landscape. Even the return of Christ and the End of Days will arrive without most ever knowing and without anyone stopping to see from where the Spirit was and is flowing. These are the ones who dismiss the journeys of others and will one day be written into the last page of His story in a way for future generations to see the error of their ways.

The followers of Moses were led blindly on faith alone for forty years. Noah built an ark when there was no rain. Abraham nearly took the life of his son in demonstration of his faith. Lot's wife was turned into a pillar of salt when she did not heed the words of the angel rescuing her at the time. That one deserves repeating, for it might just be the most relevant in the end times. While being rescued by an angel, Lot's wife still chose not to listen – and in turn, her death was written about for future generations. Daniel was thrown into a den of lions and still few chose to listen. David had to defeat a giant. The point is that the Glory of the Lord comes in all shapes and sizes, in all forms and surprises. He will speak in ways that defy logic while the ego will casually cast it aside as coincidence. The truth that many will never know should be understood as housed within the words of the journeys of others. Their complete written stories – the last pages to be read – embody the hope and inspiration that should serve as a catalyst for each person to experience the Spirit themselves; to defy all odds, to go against logic, to pray countless hours while asking to hear His voice. He will always speak – each person just has to learn to listen, like a child must learn to hear before he can begin to understand spoken words. At first, it will be senseless and without form. But, in time, words will be heard. His Voice will be heard.

All In

There is a time in everyone's life where there is a distinct decision on whether to go "all in." To some, this is a moment that arises in gambling, when a person either decides to bluff a great hand, or when he knows he has the best hand at the table and is incapable of losing, though sometimes going "all in" is a last ditch effort to remain in the game. The point is that going "all in" is rarely an action taken without great pause or consideration.

For non-gamblers, going "all in" may be seen as a passion unfolding in a certain area of desire. To achieve success, many people pour their entire being into a specific avenue in hopes that the effort will one day return great rewards. When it comes to personal ambition, going "all in" cannot be bluffed. But when it comes to relationships, this is where the concept of going "all in" is blurred somewhere between knowing the Love in and of another is unbeatable, and bluffing the way through the eventual trampling of someone's heart. There is no inbetween. The same can be said for a true relationship with God. There is only going "all in," or there is not. There are no half-truths, nothing inbetween.

Along the journey, God had pushed me beyond the bounds of my comfort zone. For an analytical mind, planning and knowing what awaits ahead is the crux of the walk through life. The mind is constantly weighing pros and cons, whys and why-nots, upward potential and the potential to fall... as did my mind. But perhaps the word "crux" is the most appropriate word to explore here, because the word "crux" is the root of the word "crucifixion" – and that word cannot be bested in description of how the analytical mind must be crucified to find faith in God along the journey. And perhaps another, even greater comparison can be made in the imagery that comes to mind when the word "crucifixion" is uttered, for most certainly the story of the life, death, and resurrection of Jesus Christ is the first thought that enters into most people's minds.

At the age of thirty, Jesus began his ministry. It was a moment he went "all in" and asked his followers to do so as well. He was baptized in a demonstration of his faith to the world. Immediately after, he fasted in the desert for forty-days, where he only relied on his faith in God for his survival. When Jesus returned from the desert and his forty-day fast, he approached Simon Peter and Andrew and asked them to follow him. Immediately, they left everything behind and followed his lead. From there, Jesus saw James and John and called upon them to follow him. Immediately they left everything behind to follow his lead. It is awe-inspiring to think what it means to truly go "all in" when tasked with performing this demonstration of faith. When reading the passages directly from the Bible, the verses portray the second grandest demonstration of faith – second only to Jesus accepting his fate to die for the sins of mankind. And in that, there is no greater demonstration of going "all in."

...

18 As Jesus was walking beside the Sea of Galilee, he saw two brothers, Simon called Peter and his brother Andrew. They were casting a net into the lake, for they were fishermen. 19 "Come, follow me," Jesus said, "and I will send you out to fish for people." 20 At once they left their nets and followed him.

21 Going on from there, he saw two other brothers, James son of Zebedee and his brother John. They were in a boat with their father Zebedee, preparing their nets. Jesus called them, 22 and immediately they left the boat and their father and followed him.

-Matthew 4:18-22

...

The day that I had my first "all in" moment along this portion of the journey began on November 25, 2011. It occurred in the wake of the previous "all ins" from the first thirty years of my life, where I had committed all I was and all I had to a marriage that withered away and a self-funded business venture that found me face down in the sand as each of my clients inexplicably went upside-down financially. The days of encumbered darkness leading into the eventual prayer to God and phone call to my cousin Bryan on that November evening should best be seen as the moment my Father helped me understand that every other previous attempt at "all ins" were really just bluffs at the card game of life. Perhaps the greatest irony was that these bluffs had fooled my own mind into thinking I had an unbeatable hand in Love and career. But it would take the house of cards falling down all around me to understand that anything *I thought I created* in the success story of my first thirty years was just a bluff to my mind – and in that I came to understand that the only unbeatable hand was held by the hand of God.

The second "all in" moment I committed to with my Father was even more defining. And, I suppose that is how each of these moments will continue to go because each new step along the journey is always bigger than the last. It will always take the preceding step as the foundation for the motion to be made to the next. Somewhere along the way, crawling becomes toddling, which becomes walking, until one day the pace of the steps and fluidity in the motion are best defined as running through the sand. In the days after returning from Ponte Vedra, my Father began to help me understand how the next portion of the Love story to be written with Lindsey as His muse, would house the sweetest celebration I would ever know. For it was after returning home that the fluidity of the conversations I had with my Father began to increase as He prepared me for the days to come.

Through hours of daily prayer, and a continued effort to demonstrate that every action I took was willfully intended to be the most pleasing unto His eyes, I sought guidance in how to move forward. The seemingly impossible situations He tasked me with each day became a greater demonstration in my faith in following His guidance. The commitment to even give the book to Lindsey seemed like the definition to going "all in," but that was really just a blurb on the cover of His book to grab my attention to the real Love story He planned to tell.

During these days, every fantasy ending to the story of Gravity Calling was entertained. The picture perfect resort that I toured in Ponte Vedra became the setting to where the contents of the safety deposit box would lead Lindsey. The financially impossible ideas suddenly were no longer impossible as I inexplicably received back payments from old clients that I had long given up on ever receiving. Tax returns yielded unexpected gains, and the promise of a new job that would allow me the flexibility to move to Florida entered into my life during these days. It was a whirlwind month to say the least – all while I waited for the call from the potter to let me know the coffee mugs were complete.

The ending to the story that my Father wanted to tell, was one of hope, of Ever-After, one of never-wanting, for all that could be desired would be prepared by His hand. I came to understand that the contents of the box were to exhibit this very demonstration to Lindsey. The box was to provide a hope that required blind faith to continue on the journey. Words were to be written, events were to be planned. Everything that was to be included was intended to wrap the soul of Lindsey around God's finger so that a gentle tug would lead her in the direction of the sun and the sand. The financial limitations I once thought existed faded into the distance. And even when it seemed the directives I was led to fulfill would exhaust the money I was inexplicably receiving, another gain would occur to take care of any potential concerns.

Crowns

For a man who literally had nothing to his name after having recently paid off the debt accrued in the aftermath of the house of cards collapsing at the age of thirty, I now saw how I had everything I would ever need. I was the richest man in the world without a dollar to my name. To see how my Father provided for everything needed while performing the tasks of His call, is an experience that can not be understood without personally experiencing the magnificence of His Love. With each step I took, I saw the Promised Land falling into view. It was not just about the destination of the Love story with Lindsey. It was about His Love and seeing just how great it can be with God as the foundation, while only following faith in His call alone.

These were the days that going "all in" became defined as bringing to life the greatest Love story ever told through the words penned by His hand. The story was no longer about the words I thought I was writing in recognition of the journey to Love. The story was much greater in scope. The story was His story, experienced through the words pouring through my hand. The promise of Ever-After and all that Lindsey would discover in the safety-deposit box was a micro example of the macro story of finding Him. This was not a Love story about me. This was a Love story about His Love. Make no mistake that every action from the point of this recognition forward, was the very definition of going "all in." To go "all in" was to tell the story that He desired to be told, the story of His Love experienced through the romance of the soul. All that He desired to include in the box, was something that I would not understand until much later. For as hindsight would require much more time to pass for knowledge to be gained, these days were intended to be a testament of faith to follow all that He commanded so that one day it could be written for others to read throughout the ages. Inside of the box, the contents would demonstrate everything ever required to understand the journey to Love, the journey to Him, the journey to Heaven on Earth, Heaven above, and the Promised Land holding all of the earthly Love she would find standing there, waiting for her in the sand.

Beauty & the Beast

Few fairytales have an ending as magnificent as Disney's Beauty and the Beast. It is possibly one of the most romantic movies ever told for adults and children alike. Few would argue that the story is one of the most warming ideals anyone in Love could ever hope to experience. But while it is a movie that has been viewed by hundreds of millions of people, few may have understood the ending for the spiritual story being told. Perhaps some may see glimmers of the story of spiritual Love through the theme's portrayal of beauty found within. Spiritual elements are cast into the storyline that may be recognizable to some. But maybe the most amazing way to view the movie – especially the ending is replacing the term "Beauty" with "Christ" and "Beast" with "Man."

True, the story is intended to be told through the portrayal of the hidden beauty of Love, but the spiritual story told beneath the visualization of the movie is what pulls on the heartstrings deep within the soul. When the movie is viewed through the perspective of "Christ and the Man," the Love story that my Father has been telling through my experiences with Lindsey is echoed in Disney's version of the story. And while I would not see my experiences with Lindsey in any comparison to the movie until nearly a year later, it was imperative that the contents of the box that Lindsey would open would tell a story in a way reminiscent to the endings of the greatest fairytale Love stories ever told throughout the ages. But in order to see where my Father was leading me with the contents, it is important to first see just how His Love story is told in "Christ and the Man." And while it may take a couple of passes at the explanation (due to new concepts being introduced) to see the truth that it holds, it truly is a beautiful story once it is revealed.

In the beginning, is important to understand that the Blu-ray and DVD versions of Beauty and the Beast contain twenty-two chapters for the movie. It is no coincidence that the oldest languages of mankind have twenty-two characters forming each respective alphabet. Each letter represents much more than a sound; each letter represents an archetypal meaning. And while this concept is the sole topic explored in Book VIII of these Books of Nine, for now it should be understood that these concepts are the heart of the language of the Divine. These twenty-two characters form the way that God communicates with each and every one of us, and how we communicate to those around us (though it has been hidden from modern man over the ages). It is part of the reason the Bible and even the Quran speak of how Divine text should not be altered, and how one day mankind will return to the original languages that predate modern man. But without going into detail (for there is much that should be explored in Book VIII by each reader), the twenty-two chapters demonstrate how the creators of the original story were telling a spiritual story all along.

The final letters that comprise the divine archetypal alphabet carry the meanings of: (19) faith, (20) hope/attain, (21) radiant Love, and (22) divinity. While each chapter in the movie corresponds with the other sequential archetypes, the final chapters are the most important to explore for this portion of the story. Chapter twenty of the movie is when Belle races back to the castle of the Beast. The Beast and Gaston (who represents man without light inside) are fighting on the rooftop of the castle. In chapter nineteen, the Beast had let Belle go with the faith (archetype 19, chapter 19) that she would one day return to him. As chapter twenty opens, all hope seems lost to the Beast, but she returns just as Gaston is about to slay him. The beast, filled with hope that Love will win over darkness, stands up and begins to fight his attacker. At this point in the battle, Gaston swings a large club at Beast, but misses and knocks the head off of a stone replica of a beast. In symbolic terms, this is the moment that demonstrates "the mind of no mind," "the headless man," the symbol of the Egyptian ankh, a halo around the head, and many other symbols that are intended to illustrate man detaching from his earthly body and surrendering to spiritual control. Filled with hope in the potential for perfect Love, it is symbolic to a person surrendering to the Love of God.

Filled with hope in Love, the beast overcomes Gaston and overcomes the loathing of his own vessel. But instead of slaying his attacker, Beast leaves Gaston alive as he turns to climb a tower to reach Belle. In this scene, it can be understood that the Beast would not murder another, but forgave him on his ascent to Belle, whose name is French for "Beauty" and who represented the perfect Love...a Love that should be understand as finding Christ within. On Beast's ascent to Love, Gaston makes one last attempt to slay him by plunging a knife into Beast's side just as Beast reached Belle and he held his hand to her face while saying, "Belle. You came back." It is possibly the most symbolic Biblical example in the movie, for this particular scene mirrors the final moments of Jesus's crucifixion. For just before Jesus ascended to Heaven, while hanging on the cross, he was stabbed in the side with a knife to ensure that he was dead.

Though Beast managed to push Gaston off of him and reach the top of the tower, Beast fell at the feet of Belle on the platform atop of the tower. Just before this chapter ends, Beast dies in Belle's arms, as she tells him how much she Loves him. At this point, Chapter twenty-one begins. It is a chapter that captures every bit of Love the movie could hope to convey. It is no coincidence that the twenty-first archetypal letter of the language of the Divine means "radiant Love" as the writers of the story wanted to demonstrate the spiritual aspect of the story in every symbolic way that could be explored. The Love demonstrated through Belle's words causes Beast to be resurrected through a transformation reminiscent to a caterpillar emerging from a cocoon as a butterfly. In this case, Beast emerges from the cape wrapped around him in a burst of light just before the world around the two of them is revealed to be a Kingdom full of angelic symbolism.

The moment the credits begin is the start of Chapter twenty-two, the last archetypal letter of the Divine language representing "completion of the circle, the arc, and divinity." In the earliest languages, these letters were represented by shapes and basic pictures. The twenty-second letter was demonstrated as a cross, symbolic of finding Christ and the completion of the circle. But perhaps it is best to take the last scene from the story, change the names around, and describe it spiritually, as that is how the writers intended it to be communicated to the soul. So here are Chapters twenty and twenty-one, written in spiritual form.

...

Christ and the Man
Chapter 20: Hope

As the chapter opens, Lucifer, who has been masquerading as an egotistical and vain man only concerned with the flesh, raises his bow and arrow to shoot the man seeking Christ in the back. The man is staring out the window, hoping that Christ will one day return, for Christ had promised He would return and be with him forever.

The man winces in pain at the feeling of being shot in the back, and has nearly lost all hope in Christ's return. Lucifer pushes him out of the window and down to the edge of the roof where the man just stares down below, unwilling to fight back. Lucifer exclaims, "What's the matter, too kind and gentle to fight back?" Lucifer breaks off a piece of the roof in the shape of a rod and hold it above his head, ready to bring the man's life to an end.

Just at this moment, Christ's voice is heard. "Nooooo!!!!!!"

The man looks out and sees Christ returning to him riding on a white horse, just as it was foretold in Revelation. The man cries out, "Messiah!!!!"

Christ shouts back to Lucifer, "Nooo! Lucifer! No!" He then signals to His white horse to ascend to the top of the tower.

Invigorated by the Messiah's return, the man turns around and catches the rod being swung at him by Lucifer. The fight ensues with the man overpowering Lucifer long enough to run over to a safer place to fight. Lucifer swings his rod erratically, knocking the head off of a statue of a man. It is in this moment it is demonstrated that the man Lucifer is fighting is not the same as other men. This man has surrendered to Christ, filled by His Love, and is now led by the Spirit of God.

Lucifer turns to taunting, since he cannot find the man among the statues of men on the roof. Lucifer cries out to the man, "Come on out and fight! Did you think you found the Love of Christ? Did you honestly think Christ would Love you when I exist?"

Those words were enough to provoke the man out of hiding to continue fighting Lucifer. Confident that he would overcome the man since the man responded to his taunt, Luci-

Beauty & the Beast

fer says, "It is over beast. You will never have Christ." But just as Lucifer thinks he has defeated the man, the man lifts Lucifer up by the neck and holds him out over the abyss.

Lucifer pleads with the man, "Put me down. Put me down. Please, don't hurt me! I'll do anything! Anything!" The man sees how small and pathetic Lucifer is and begins to feel compassion for Lucifer's soul. Instead of throwing Lucifer into the abyss, he pulls him back on to the roof as a demonstration of Christ's dominance and Love. He shouts at Lucifer, "Get Out!"

With Lucifer huddled in defeat, the man turns his back on him and continues his ascent to Christ, who is waiting for him at the top of the tower. Christ calls out the man's name to let him know he is there waiting for him. The man shouts back, "Messiah!" in recognition.

Just as the man reaches Christ and they hold hands, Lucifer makes one last attempt to prevent the man from finding the Love of Christ. Lucifer pulls out a knife, leaps and plunges it into the man's side in an attempt to take his life. Though the knife gashed the side of the man, Lucifer's efforts caused him to fall to his demise in the abyss.

The man turned back to Christ and with his last efforts, reached the landing at the top of the tower. As Christ held the man in his arms, the man struggled to say his last words. The man held his hand to Christ's face and said in near disbelief as he was overcome with Love, "You…you came back."

With tears in His eyes, Christ said, "Of course I came back. I couldn't let them… Oh! This is all my fault. If only I had gotten here sooner." Christ could not bear the thought of His children suffering as He had to suffer during His crucifixion.

The man was now in full recognition of the spiritual moment and responded with every bit of strength in spiritual words under his dying earthly breath, "Maybe it's better, it's better this way."

Christ, with tears falling down His face as he watched His child's earthly body die in His arms said, "Don't talk like that. You'll be alright. We're together now. Everything's gonna be fine. You'll see."

The man's final words spoken were, "At least I got to see you one last time." With that, his earthly body collapsed onto the ground as Christ wept over his body. Christ saw all of the Love the man had for Him and was overcome with sorrow. He said, "No. No. Please. Please. Please don't leave me. I Love you" as he lay His head on the man's chest and sobbed.

Chapter 21: Love

As Christ and the angels wept around the man, the spirit of God poured down on him. The man's purple cape wrapped around him like a caterpillar entering into a cocoon. As cyan-colored rain poured down around them and smoke of cyan hue filled the periphery, the man was resurrected before everyone's eyes. The cyan color is the color of the sphere of God's Kingdom, hidden from earthly eyes. As the man transformed before everyone looking on, light raced through his body, and began to burst out his fingertips and toes. The light filling his body was Christ filling him within. His earthly body was transformed into the perfect form that the Love of Christ once knew.

When he stood before the Love of Christ, He reached His hand to the resurrected man's face. The man said, "Messiah, it is me." The Messiah put His hand to the face of the man and studied his face in a gesture symbolic to how Mary and the disciples reacted when they saw Jesus Christ resurrected. While the man's earthly form was no more, his soul was pure and recognizable to Him. And though his form was now different, the Messiah exclaimed to the man, "It is you!" just before the Resurrection Ceremony began.

The man and Christ are united in a whirlwind of fireworks and celebration for everyone to see. The castle transforms before man's eyes into the Kingdom. Heaven and Earth become One as man had found the Love of Christ within, which lifted the veil separating perfection and man's sin. The demons and gargoyles that adorned the earthly castle were transformed into angels and divine creations. The guardians that the man saw the spirit speaking through (though others would think he was crazy for entertaining that notion) transformed from the candlestick, clock, and pot into the angels they were all along. And isn't it symbolic that the guardians to the man were represented by "time," "light," and "a pot made of clay?"

As everyone was revealed in their true form on God's Grand Stage, the guardians all shouted out and greeted each other in a warm embrace. The angel named Lumiere, who represented the essence of Love through the light of candlelight, shouts out for all to hear, "It is a miracle!" just before the scene cuts to the grand ballroom And though the next aspect of the description may not make complete sense until the end of Book III, the man and Christ within should best be seen as Adam and Eve, who waltz in a grand ballroom, unique and different in identity to every other angel and couple in the room, though united in the perfect Love of the first man and the first woman, just as God always intended it to be.

Before the scene fades out, the child companion represented by a smaller clay vessel throughout the earthly man's life turns to his angelic mother and asks, "Are they gonna live happily ever after mama?" She replies, "Of course my dear. Of course," just before the scene cuts to all of the angels watching the newly united couple dance together, as they fell in perfect Love. As they danced, the most beautiful of Love song of all time begins to play. The lyrics pick up at a later verse in the song, symbolic to the portion of the journey they were now on:

...

"Certain as the sun, rising in the east
Tale as old as time, song as old as rhyme
Beauty and the beast
Tale as old as time, song as old as rhyme
Beauty and the Beast"

...

Beauty & the Beast

As the song begins to reach its end and the camera slowly pulls away from the couple dancing among the angels in the grand ballroom, a stained glass window fills the screen. As the camera continues to pull out to reveal the entire stained glass portrait, it can be seen that the story of Christ and the Man is bound together in the most beautiful stained-glass pattern held within the wall of a cathedral. Angels surround the window on either side, while God looks down on them from above. The story of one man's journey in search of Christ is captured in the glass of a stained-glass window, where light can pour through and tell the story for all time. As the image of the stained glass window fades out, the credits begin to role...the beginning of Chapter 22: Divinity.

...

There is no sweeter ending to a Love story, than the one told in Beauty and the Beast. And though the form of the story that was just told is most likely not the one that is seen with earthly eyes when watching the movie, it is the story told for spiritual eyes to see. When spiritual eyes have been opened and the world is seen in this manner, everything – every interaction, every story told – reveals the true Love story that our Father has been telling all along. And though this may be the first story that reveals His artful approach, this is the way the world must be seen in order for Heaven and Earth to become One.

So as I continued to chase Love through Gravity Calling and the fairytale ending I hoped would come true, I can now see in hindsight how I was the Beast and Lindsey, God's muse.

Crowns

I was blissfully unaware of the greater story He intended to tell all along, though every action I was called to make still held an earthly truth. I can now see there is no better way for Him to reveal how Heaven and Earth become One than to demonstrate the story through a man chasing Love upon the Earth. The actions I was called to take in bringing the fairytale ending to life, were meant to resemble how a man would find the Love of Christ. But at the time I was to experience this portion of the journey, I could only see the story for the overwhelming abundance of Love pouring through.

I saw it through the potential of Love with Lindsey and how the potential for Ever-After was unfolding. I saw it through the inexplicable way everything I was tasked to purchase and arrange was covered financially. I saw it through the writings I had been led to complete. I saw it through the experiences in the heavens and conversations with His angels. But most importantly, I saw a fairytale ending coming to life, through all that I was tasked to place in the box for Lindsey to find. In all of the ways I could never have imagined, in the future chapters of the story God planned to reveal, the most romantic story I would ever experience was placed under lock and key in a safety deposit box at His will.

The Grand Ballroom

To tell a Love story of any kind requires a spiritual element of the unseen. Though I could explain how every action in life must be taken with this same approach – housed in the unimpeded, fluent actions of the bodily vessel – the care to adhere to respect and embrace these elements in a Love story is the most important of all. People upon the Earth rarely see beyond the physical. Some hope and believe in the potential for the unseen, but hope has mostly become lost among the remnant of battered emotions caused by Lucifer's army. The glimmers of hope available for the masses to see is housed in the embodiment of earthly Love. Some may say, "What about the churches? What about faith?" But, while there are most certainly glimmers to those who know where to look, to others lost on God's playground, each church appears to be just another fraternity fighting to tell everyone why they should feel special to be selected by their respective congregations and how "becoming a pledge" will forever change their lives.

These words are not intended to take away from the various religions and churches across the Earth. Rather, it is intended to demonstrate a truth in how the smoldering landscape of desolation must look to those barely hanging on to hope. To those who have already lost hope, the landscape must appear desolate and unforgiving. For those people who are approached upon a fight-for-survival landscape, red flags must arise as there must be something in it for the ones who approached. This is the ugly truth of how a lost soul must see the Earth and how those who think they are found have been falsely mislead, for Christ's reign upon the Earth has not yet begun.

But it is the will of our Father to unite the world in Love. For Love is the Universal Law that binds Heaven and Earth. Again, to some this may sound like a repeat of the hippy movement in the past. Others may hear the word "Love" and cringe at the implications. However, these words are not instructions for the world to become lost in the lust of others, nor attempt to experience earthly Love in lieu of our Father. Instead, these words are intended to illustrate a greater message – how His Love transcends Heaven and Earth through the feelings of Love erupting.

The first time a person falls in Love is a moment he will never forget. And perhaps it is the reason why many become so jaded to Love after a broken heart. The fall from the top of such an elated feeling, leaves a crater from the impact since there is no graceful way to land from such a great distance. But the Love of the Father is a Love that never dies, though those who "think" they have found His Love may deceive others with their lies. To experience the true Love by spiritual definition, one must have surrendered to Him completely. This means the removal of the mind from controlling decisions and, instead, always unquestionably following His lead. In the

The Grand Ballroom

beginning it will be tough, as it will become the mind's greatest battle in accepting the stumbles that will happen in learning how to follow. To those who "want it all" immediately, failure will be met quickly upon the journey since the emotion of "wanting" is tied to the ego. For those who fail, they may turn their backs, but it is up to every other brother and sister to help them redirect.

So how can such a story of His Love be told with all of the fraternal divisions? The only common ground is through the story of Love told in such a way that it evokes tugs upon the heartstrings of the soul. A Love story is the only method that can reach every brother and sister upon His playground, for Love is the constant that brings forth existence. Even the most jaded person will feel the ripples of the story, for Love's impact transcends throughout eternity. And while a jaded person may not want to witness the sight of Love or hear about Love directly, the ripples will reverberate through others who will tell the story in a way that can be handled. It is the same delicacy in how a hockey player learns to hit a puck properly by sliding an egg down the ice, for the greatest skill in strength is the delivery through grace. To onlookers of a hockey match, it would appear at the surface level as only a brawny, testosterone-filled sport being fought between two foes. Little do they know how so much power in the hits and speed on the skates are centered on the concepts of delicacy and grace. And so therein, the story of how our Father's Love awaits each and every one of us can be understood through the perfected delivery and craft of a Love story's words.

Crowns

Upon the journey that I had embarked on while blindly following the words written by my Father's hand, I was faced with a series of tasks to ensure His Story was told in a way for Everyman. The ending was to embody the fairytale story that every child has heard – the one that ends with Love conquering all as the credits fade in. So as I received my instructions, I set off to accomplish His tasks. Confined by only the time of Lindsey's work schedule and her children's school, everything else was wide open in both scope and potential. With the knowledge of the limitations I had in her schedule – I began there, by finding out when spring break was for her children. Once the time period fell into view, I understood how His story would be told – all in a way that would pull at the heartstrings of her soul. It is important that I did not say heart, for that would imply only an earthly Love was involved. For this story embodies a Spiritual Love, and through that, a divine communication between souls was to take place – a communication where I only served as a vessel for His words to pour through to her soul.

Once I understood the timing to her children's spring break, I now had all I needed for His ending to be written. I prayed and sought guidance on the dates that I should meet Lindsey in a coffee shop to deliver Gravity Calling as well as for the rest of the events to play out once she had completed reading the book. And while many of the circumstances and ways that my Father guided me during this time would not make much sense for the reader, these were the days that I continued to learn to hear His voice and understand His inten-

The Grand Ballroom

tions. I came to see that His plan involved a literal interpretation to the ending of Gravity Calling. In the final chapters of the book, it is revealed that "[the story] would end with me standing with my earthly feet buried in the physical sand here on Earth, but one last great chapter remained." This was in reference to the theme of my journey traversing across the desert sands in a metaphorical version of Numbers with Deuteronomy remaining ahead.

With this recognition, I booked flights for her and her two children to arrive in Jacksonville, Florida on the Friday her children got out for Spring Break on March 28th, returning late on Sunday evening, March 30th. As a demonstration of faith in my Father's directive, I booked the flights as non-refundable.

The next days involved planning the perfect version of the journey she was to embark upon as I would wait for her arrival with my feet in the sands of the beaches of Florida. During these days, there were no financial limitations. Everything that I prayed for guidance upon was met with the finances to provide for its inclusion in the story. Even the three round-trip plane tickets were paid for by the grace of His hand. The fantasy weekend getaways to the resort in Ponte Vedra became a reality as I was able to schedule a version of paradise for her arrival. But, for the story to be told as a journey for her to discover all that was ahead, the plans had to multiply to include accommodations for her children in the midst of the fairytale ending. It was important for her children to experience a glance at the Promised Land in such a way that did not overwhelm them or turn them away. I booked three separate rooms at the beachfront resort for the weekend. Two rooms would adjoin for her and her children (who were both teenagers). My room would be on the other side of the resort, to separate the two sides of the story and to not cause any discomfort in the trip. Everything about the destination was intended to be a paradise getaway to begin getting to know each other outside of the church setting.

For the second day of the trip, I reserved a private dinner at a restaurant that required formal cocktail attire. I knew I would have to accommodate for this requirement without giving away the plans for the weekend, so I again sought guidance from my Father. I was led to understand the story was to unfold in a way symbolic to the way the angels had guided me along the way. It was to be the earthly version of an angelic-escorted visit to the heavens. In order to take care of the formal attire requirement, I met with both managers at Nordstrom in Green Hills Mall to arrange the surprise that was in store for Lindsey. I shared with both managers the story of Gravity Calling and how Lindsey would be reading the ending in the coming weeks. They were both overcome with happiness and joy in the moment. They told me how they wanted to help make it the most perfect ending to the story possible.

We decided that one of the items that she would discover in the box, would lead her to the store where the managers would have prepared a room for her with a variety of dresses and shoes for the events planned. Money was not an object in

The Grand Ballroom

making sure Lindsey had the perfect attire that she desired. But since Lindsey would be tasked with going to Nordstrom on blind faith, I did not want her to fear not having the money to purchase a dress. So, the managers and I decided to include a gift card in the box as well. Though it would likely cover the attire the managers recommended, I let them know that if her clothes cost more, they could call me and I would take care of the balance. I purchased a $500 gift card and left with a peace in knowing they would be able to help her while keeping the events that awaited a secret. I only shared with the managers what they needed to know. The rest of the story was for Lindsey to experience on her own.

With that portion of the next steps planned, I returned to scheduling a series of other events at the resort. Knowing perfectly well that this would be a time for us to catch up on old times – and if nothing else, to have a good time as friends – everything planned still had to be prepared in a way for romance or friends. I spoke with the management of the Spa at the resort and shared with them the story unfolding. We decided on a half-day package that would be everything she could ever want. It was possible that I would not even tell her about the Spa, but it needed to be scheduled in the event everything worked out as planned. It was another non-refundable expense, but it was again part of the story to be told.

When I visited the resort and fantasized about the most romantic getaway possible, I toured the ballrooms and the various locations on the resort where there were Grand Pianos. Since this was to be the most perfect fairytale ending possible,

Crowns

I spoke with the managers of the resort to see if they would allow me to book the Grand Ballroom. Though they said they never book or allow visitors into the ballroom unless a conference has booked the facilities, they agreed once I shared with them the story of the book. It was again part of the ending to be told, but in no way should it be understood that this was the one and only version of the ending. At this point, I had to plan for the perfect romance, offset for the unexpected, and have a foundation of a perfect first-time experience with each other outside of church.

I booked one of Jacksonville's best pianists – again a non-refundable effort. I shared with her the story that I hoped would be told. I included a set list that included some of the songs I knew she liked as well as many of my favorite romantic songs – all of them purely instrumental in the style of Jim Brickman. I coordinated her arrival at the resort with the managers and was comforted that all would be taken care of with their highest level of service. And while there were many other items to purchase, to prepare, and events to coordinate to provide the polish for telling the most perfect Love story ever written, the most important items to mention are the hundreds of frosted-glass hurricane candle holders, accompanying candles, tiki torches, the gallons of fuel required for the tiki torches, both fake and real rose petals, a handcrafted stand for candles to be placed, and a perfect stained glass box – which was symbolic to the stained glass pattern that had been rebuilt on the journey to Love. The contents of the stained

The Grand Ballroom

glass box should best be understood as the promise of Ever-After, though only to be revealed if it was God's will.

Whether she would see the whole story in its most romantic story ever experienced, or whether she would only see the story as a weekend getaway and some time away from Nashville were the polarizing accommodations that had to be made. The fluidity to the transition between the extremes was the journey I was to experience as the motion of two souls being drawn together moved whimsically around while my earthly feet remained in the sand. I made plans for a driver to pick her and her children up at the airport to take them to the resort. The driver was none other than my father, though that would not be revealed until the end. For how much more symbolic of a gesture could be made than having my Father bring Love together with Lindsey following on blind faith to a destination unknown as my feet remained in the sand awaiting the Promised Land?

If everything were to play out in a picture of perfection, when Lindsey arrived, she would be escorted to her room by the hotel staff. She would find a letter in an unbleached envelope sealed with red wax, stamped with the letter L. The letter inside the envelope would explain to her that the events of the weekend were to be viewed as if her life from Nashville was placed on pause. She would be instructed that an hour after her arrival, she would receive a knock on her door from the hotel staff to escort her to her next location. She was instructed to bring an envelope she would have found in the safety deposit box that was also in an unbleached envelope with a red wax seal with the letter L stamped in the wax.

Though she would not know where the hotel staff would lead her, she would be taken to a location on the beach perfectly between our three rooms – a number symbolic of the center point of the Trinity. The beach would be lighted with hundreds of candles in frosted-hurricane candle holders and tiki torches. There would be seven tiki torches in the middle, representing God's signature. In front of the tiki torches, I would be waiting for her wearing a white linen shirt and suit, barefoot with my feet in the sand.

Knowing full and well that her arrival would be met with a demonstration of abundance, I would rely on passive wit and humor to calm her nerves. We would begin by exchanging envelopes – hopefully with both having remained sealed. There were actually two variations of the letter included in the envelope I would be holding. Based on how I gauged her response in meeting at the beach, I would pick which version of the story would begin to be told for the evening. I would then ask her to open the envelope and read the letter. This particular letter contained a chapter entitled "The Heavens Stood Still." It was almost a real-time version of the events she was experiencing and was to be included as the next to last chapter of the version of Gravity Calling that would eventually be published.

After she finished reading her letter, I would open the envelope in my hands and read the words to the final chapter of the book. It was important for her to see that the ending of the

The Grand Ballroom

story was written before she arrived, but was always held in her hands. The final chapter was entitled "Love Always" and wrapped up the story of a perfect Love – a spiritual Love – one that transcends the bounds of time and space. The ending would not change, regardless of how the events played out over the weekend or which envelope she was handed when she arrived on the beach, for the story my Father intended to tell always ended with His Love as the destination. Neither chapter would cause the weekend to be overly romantic if we were to only take baby steps, for the entire gesture on the beach was revealed as a demonstration of the spiritual journey and how the book's ending would be penned.

Depending on how everything would go, the remainder of the weekend could transform into Ever-After with the two of us dancing to the music played live by a pianist in a candle-filled Grand Ballroom. It was an ending symbolic to the previous chapter written, where "Christ and the Man" faded out to a dance of perfect Love between Adam and Eve in God's Grand Ballroom. Though any comparison drawn to Beauty & the Beast was not revealed to me until nearly a year later into the journey as this book was written (it was the last of the nine books to be completed). But there was also another portion of the story Lindsey could experience if the events unfolded in this perfect beauty and Love. For just as Beauty & the Beast ended with a stained-glass window telling the story of a perfect Love in the picture of broken glass, the contents inside of the stained-glass box would be revealed to her in the Grand Ballroom while echoing those exact same sentiments. For those with wondering minds, let's just say that my Father provided a potential for both of us to never have any wants for the rest of all time – a gesture held in symbolic nature, that will only be fully revealed according to His time. And just as the scene of stained glass is the final scene in Beauty & the Beast before the credits begin at Chapter 22, so to would stained glass be presented in the final scene in the weekend with Lindsey.

For the final day she would spend in Paradise would be experienced with just herself and her children alone, knowing the promise of Ever-After and the demonstration of God's Love was no longer just a fairytale filled with hope. It was real, and was experienced in her time in the sand and the sun. It would be the most perfect presentation of Heaven on Earth. But before the events of the weekend could ever begin to unfold into this version of perfection or some version in-between, she would first have to find the key and open the box to find the contents to guide her there. When she arrived she would find the letter following, awaiting her in her room. It was these words that would guide her soul to meet mine while I stood with my feet in the sand on the shores of His Promised Land.

...

Lindsey,

As you've probably come to realize by this point, nothing about this weekend will be ordinary. It is my hope that each moment from this point forward will be approached with a blind eye to the past where only the present experience exists. Just imagine this weekend as if your previous life was placed on pause when you boarded the plane to Jacksonville, where

The Grand Ballroom

only the world as it exists in this very moment is to be experienced for all that it is, and all that it could be.

I hope you and your children find the accommodations welcoming. As you have come to realize, you have a separate adjoining suite from your children and will have both of those suites throughout the weekend. In approximately an hour from your arrival, you will receive a knock at your door from one of the hotel staff. He/she will escort you to your next destination before dinner. For this, it just needs to be you and the sealed envelope you were asked to bring with you. Don't forget to bring that. Your children can continue getting ready for dinner (casual clothes). Don't worry. They will be fine and you will be back for them in a short time.

...

Tonight, as you get ready – just assume casual/nice dress. This is not the evening that requires the cocktail dress...save that for tomorrow.

Always,
Jonathan

Trimmed In Red

It seemed like barely any days had passed from the first time my eyes would meet Lindsey's to the day that that had now arrived at this point along the journey. Though at this point it was only a tale told between two souls with a large gap of time separating us from any type of fairytale Love coming true. The point I first saw the lightning that ignited the room to when we would see each other again, was a song held in silence though my soul was constantly humming along to her tune. To her, perhaps in the wake of her previous relationship ending, she would only see our paths crossing as two old acquaintances entertaining a familiar melody of an old song. Or perhaps she would see the promise of forever wrapped up in the song playing in the background when we see each other again.

Wherever her heart would be discovered when she would read the words of Gravity Calling, had to be understood by me as the point of origin for the rest of the story remaining to be told. I was marching along to the rhythm of the Grand Conductor, knowing all along that every step she would be asked to take had to be in sync to the very same rhythm. Her call to action had to be packaged up and tailored in a way that was inviting to her eyes, and not be seen as overwhelming or overbearing. To be honest, most of it was to be hidden, with only words guiding her along to each next destination. It was a real-world version of a "Choose Your Own Adventure" book, the kind that was popular when I was a child, where every choice she would make would ripple through every successive chapter of these books – an ending crafted with the melody of her heart's will.

Though it was only becoming faintly apparent at this point along my journey, I was beginning to see how all of my actions demonstrated a modern version of the movement of God's Spirit. My Father's directives in the delivery of this Love story, was no different than His Love Story that came before it. For the very essence of His Love Story written through every word of the Bible and through other various religious texts, holds an even greater truth and promise than would be placed at Lindsey's fingertips. But they would mirror the same ideal, and held the potential for His Ever-After at the mercy of freewill. For how could He tell the world of a Love so grand, where everything on Earth pales in comparison to the Promised Land? It is actually quite simple. He would tell the story through those who came before, those who are, and those who will one day be. For His Story of finding His Love is no mystery. It is spelled out with instructions in the written testimonies of those who found His Love throughout the ages before us, but sometimes He needs to help guide others through another map, another inspired story, or even through the birth of a child – another Child, His Child. He tells the story every day, in every way, for every man, woman, and child – tailored in a way that is not overbearing and requires only a soul's freewill to seek Ever-After and leave behind the mundane of earthly fill.

Our Father's Love is the grandest Love of all and is delivered to each of us upon a platter through the testimonies of others. From whatever perspective each person views the world, there is an aspect of His truth within arms' reach. So as I would begin to see the importance of perspective, I understood the contents of the safety deposit box would need to be tailored to any possible expectation. For in whatever lens of perspective Lindsey viewed the words written, the rest of the story had to unfold in the way tailored to her decisions. With all of the plans made ranging from a waltz in the Grand Ballroom type of fairytale ending, to a weekend of rekindled spirits escaping Nashville together, the words and items Lindsey would find in the safety deposit box had to carry hope in the feelings where she placed her faith.

When Lindsey would reach the bank she was instructed to ask for Sara, who would escort her to the safety deposit box that had been reserved for her. The number of the safety deposit box and the number stamped on her key reduce-summed to seven, though that detail was unplanned and just added polish to the story. When she would pull the box out, she would see resting at the top, a crème colored envelope trimmed in red with "Read First" written upon the label. Inside of the envelope was a letter typed upon linen paper, signed in ink at the bottom with my signature. Beneath the letter, was an unbleached 9" x 12" envelope, wax-sealed in red

Crowns

and stamped with the letter L. Beneath that envelope was a smaller 6" x 9" unbleached envelope which was closed without wax. Inside of this particular envelope were two Thank-You sized cards in smaller, individual envelopes labeled for their respective purposes as well as an envelope containing the plane tickets. The two smaller envelopes contained gift cards and handwritten explanations for their respective purposes. The other two items she would find in the box were an unbroken coffee mug identical to the one she was asked to shatter as well as an identical version of the bookmark she was asked to cut open. All materials – the envelopes, the wax seal, the pens used, and the paper – were chosen with utmost care for the polish of the presentation. All in all, there were seven objects included – three in the envelope that would lead her to the destination.

As the chapters penned by her very actions were to be used as the ending to Gravity Calling, it is only appropriate that the reader be able to experience everything as she saw it – the book, the poem, all that could remain ahead, and the words that would lead her there – all are important. But, for her, there would be no prior knowledge of the potential that awaited. She would only find these words in the letter held in the envelope trimmed in red.

...

Lindsey,

Inside of this box you will find several items. First thing's first. Sorry about having you break that coffee mug. I actually liked it a lot when I had it made, so I had the potter make two. Don't worry. You won't have to break this one. This one is actually meant to drink from and use however you see fit. You will also find in this box another bookmark – this one with the fabric still intact on the back. It contains the same poem inside and you won't ever have to unstitch this one. I know it had one of your favorite verses on it, so I wanted to make sure you had one with the original intention of my soul's voice held within it. Now onto the good part.

There are two envelopes inside of this box. One is much larger than the other one and will contain a seal to ensure it remains unbroken. Do not open this envelope. There is a purpose, but for now it must remain sealed. Held within the smaller envelope, you will find three plane tickets for you and your children as well as a couple of gift cards marked for their intended purposes. One gift card is to cover your airport parking. The other gift card is for you to buy something new to wear on the day of your flight. My initial thought was for it to be used for a dress and shoes – but please use it as your heart desires. Your flight will depart after you get off work this upcoming Friday. Make sure you give yourself enough time to check in with the personal information I did not have available for you and your kids when I purchased the tickets. When you arrive in Jacksonville, a driver will be waiting for you and your family. He will have your phone number in the event of any mix-ups or mishaps. He will take you to your destination. Make sure you bring the sealed envelope with you. That part is important.

Now I know there is probably a whirlwind of thoughts tossing, tumbling, and rambling through you mind. Trust me when I say this – just breathe. There is nothing to be nervous about. If anything, writing a 300+ page book in the manner that has been done should have been where any nerves would reside, and I am perfectly at peace knowing my soul is

Crowns

naked in the words I have written — the words that, until now, have only been revealed in song silent. If anxiety exists, place it at bay and know there is nothing more I will do — nothing more unexpected that will be revealed — other than for me to be standing in the sand, awaiting your arrival. And as you are reading this, I am already there.

Always,
Jonathan

Waltzed With Her Soul

The closing minutes of Beauty and the Beast end with a transformed Beast – now a prince – dancing in the arms of a perfect Love. The two souls spin each other around across a black and white checkered dance floor, as they waltz in the castle's Grand Ballroom, surrounded by a crowd watching them fall in Love. It is a comparison I never intended to make to the events of this story, though it is possibly one of the most romantic examples of a perfect Love. The destination that awaited Lindsey in Florida could very well end with such a similar circumstance, or it could go the way of a more subtle demonstration of a spiritual Love that transcends time and space.

The angels in Heaven must have sensed my awe and wonder in the grandeur of such a gesture of Love, for I could only imagine that the Grand Ballroom would be filled with their presences, though remaining unseen. Such a thought dancing through my mind and through my prayers must have reverberated in form through the heavens to their own eyes and ears. On March 11th, just after I had scheduled a time with Lindsey to meet at a coffee shop during the upcoming weekend with my daughter, the angels took my soul to the heavens for one of my most amazing experiences I had had up to this date.

In the previous chapters of this book (as well as in Gravity Calling), I have shared just a few examples of my experiences with the angels and the heavens. But at this point along the journey, my experiences with the angels, conversations with God, and even having my soul taken to the heavens, were occurring at a clip faster than sounds legitimately possible until having read and understood the entire journaled accounts included in these Books of Nine. The journal entries are the subject matter of Books IV – VII and can be read independently from the first three books, or in succession afterwards. Rather than explain how the experience unfolded on the morning of March 11th, I have included the journal entry which was written just after the experience occurred.

...

March 11, 2014

I had a very difficult time meditating and even sleeping last night. I obviously have had a whirlwind of thoughts running through my mind – but it is disappointing that I was not able to calm the storm of thoughts last night for a prolonged period of time. However, there was one moment that I can recount with some clarity. I, again, was allowed to find the company of Lindsey's soul in the early hours of this morning. We danced to music played by a pianist. At one point, the pianist began to play "Her Man" by Gary Allen. When she noticed the song, Lindsey stopped dancing and looked at me. It was as if she queued into the moment and achieved a

Waltzed With Her Soul

state of lucidity and awareness of her surroundings. Prior to that, it was as if we were just two groggy souls dancing.

But it was at this moment when she looked at me and asked, "Is this 'Her Man?'" I said that it was. She looked at me confused. It was as if she was trying to rationalize everything going on. She fought with the idea for a moment that "Her Man" was being played while she tried to understand where she was standing. I am not sure of the significance of that particular song in her life, but at this point I have to believe that it holds an access point to special memories for her. As she looked at me, I continued to give her confidence that we were indeed dancing to "Her Man." I even hummed along to it. She leaned back in and rested her face on my right shoulder/chest. We continued dancing slowly to the music as the angels stood around us, watching us fall in Love.

...

The experience of dancing with Lindsey in the heavens is indescribable in earthly words. Every aspect of the moment was rooted on one breathtaking pillar stacked upon another. To describe the heavens is almost impossible. To describe the Love felt in the presence of angels…there are no words. To describe being in the presence of a person's soul from Earth is yet another ineffable moment. But to have all of these moments happening at once, with the experience of falling in Love while slow-dancing before the angels, is truly indescribable.

Though the journaled accounts of the heavens begin in Book IV with smaller extrapolations of the moments, the later experiences become much more detailed. This particular experience fell at a time when the entries were still shorter in length. I truly had no idea how to explain the moment, and even in hindsight as this chapter is written, words cannot do the moment justice. It was every fairytale happily-ever-after experienced at once. It was a moment I was able to experience a tangible version of Beauty and the Beast but experienced through the spiritual version of Christ and the Man. And perhaps that is why it was important for me to understand in hindsight just how the Disney classic carried such a spiritual meaning – for perhaps that is how it must be illustrated for the reader to see it from the eyes through which I see.

The morning after I was blessed to have this experience, I called the pianist I had hired for the trip to Ponte Vedra. I knew in this moment the importance of having "Her Man" played as one of the songs for us to dance to in the Grand Ballroom. Though I did not know how the song held meaning for Lindsey (or even if it did), it was important to be played for the potential. What if she were to recall "a dream of her dancing with me" – even if she chose not to say it? What if her soul would hear the song even if her mind did not? There are many mysteries to the way in which God works. As I have learned along the journey, it is not important to try to understand "why" or "how," it is only important to follow His lead. The rest will always unfold in the way He intends it is to be seen.

Days would pass, and the song would eventually be confirmed by the pianist while other details were ironed out with the resort. The weekend approaching was the weekend Lindsey and I were to meet for coffee. It was a weekend I had my daughter, and though I had never introduced her to any other

Waltzed With Her Soul

women in my life, this time would be different. For just as God was teaching me how to hear His voice, I was helping my daughter learn how to see. It was a time that my Father helped me understand that my daughter was intended to see a demonstration of my faith in the journey to Love through His voice. Lindsey had continued to tell me how she wanted to meet my daughter. And though scheduling did not work out when I had my daughter several weeks prior, Lindsey assured me she wanted to see her this weekend when we were to meet for coffee.

When the day arrived, my daughter was extremely excited to meet her. For so long, my daughter has wanted nothing more than for me to be happy. She must have noticed how I talked about Lindsey, or maybe it was in the way that my daughter would be involved. My daughter already knew about the book and the plans with the key in the coffee mug and the poem in the bookmark. She even wanted to be part of the plan by telling Lindsey that she wanted to give her the bookmark (and not me). Some may question why I would have included my daughter at all, but that is answered in the journaled accounts in the books to come. At this time, it is only important to see how God was using this experience to help my daughter learn to see.

The day we were to meet Lindsey, I sent her a text confirming that we were on our way to the coffee shop. My daughter and I arrived a little early and waited. She drank hot chocolate and I had my usual coffee. It was a time we were able to share in a wonderful father-daughter conversation. My daughter was then eight years old and as any parent would be able to identify with, this was the age where it seemed she, at times, was wiser with worldly advice than me. And perhaps she was. Perhaps she is. Perhaps that is the beauty of a child's vision. As the time passed, we soaked in every moment, talking about the Love story unfolding.

The minutes passing by as we waited for Lindsey turned into a quarter past the hour, half-past the hour, and eventually crossed over to an hour past the time we had agreed upon meeting. While my daughter and I waited, I sent a text checking up to make sure she was on her way or that we had not mixed up the location. It was important that the approach remained casual. But even so, it was met with no response. Though I was strongly conscientious of not becoming blind to earthly signs, I feared the worst and hoped for the best this time. This was possibly one of the hardest moments I have ever experienced with my daughter because she was so genuinely excited to meet Lindsey, and I felt like a failure in front of her. She knew all that was involved in the book and how this was the day that God had instructed me to give her the book. The only peace I could find was knowing, at worst, this was a testament to my faith and how my Father would see my Love.

In so many different aspects along the journey, I had experienced Lucifer's attempted obstructions. Even in Gravity Calling, His attempts were very evident, though there had not been an opportunity of this magnitude. It was a time I was beginning to better understand how the pendulum of life is always influenced by light or darkness and not by man's decision. And though to earthly eyes, the obvious assessment was that we were stood up, the part that continued to confound me was why would she have agreed to meet – especially with my daughter involved? Too many things did not make earthly sense, but in spiritual terms, I had no doubt of the reason.

My daughter and I waited for another hour and a half. But when I was ready to leave, she actually urged me to stay. She wanted me to not give up on God and demonstrate that I truly believed in all that I thought He was saying to me. She had hope when I was losing faith. It was possible that I had misinterpreted the date, but as my journals will show, that was hardly the case. After a couple more attempts to check up on Lindsey, she finally texted me back with an apology. It is hard to say whether I believed her words, even in how the sincerity in her response bled through, for without words it was obvious there was resistance.

Throughout the evening I prayed for next steps. And though I did not bring anything else up to my daughter regarding Lindsey, my daughter continued to offer me advice of what I should do next. The following day when I drove her back to her mother, she continued to bring up the subject. The question she continued to ask was not whether further effort would be made with Lindsey, but rather whether I would still give her the book that had been written. As it seemed that the action of giving the book to her was my Father's primary directive, my daughter and I debated if that could be His whole intention. Could it be that she was supposed to see my soul through the words written versus a person who had written a story? Could it be that regardless of the outcome, it was just another test of my faith in my Father? For if I had been tasked to write 300+ pages over the last several years of inexplicable heavenly encounters, what would it say to Him if I just gave up on the effort? What would it mean about the experience of the angels watching our souls fall in Love? What would it mean to say, "I understand Lucifer is involved. He can have this one…"?

The questions teetered on the edge of my own sanity. I had never felt more stretched to my emotional and rational limits before this day. After I dropped my daughter off with her mother, with a fragile heart I prayed about the landscape of possibilities. The wisdom of my daughter had poured through our conversation – or maybe a better way to say it is that she was a vessel for the Spirit. Her questions raised new questions within. How much of this weekend was a test, or did this portion of the journey actually reach its end? And if the journey had reached its end, what could possibly have been the purpose, or did ego allow me to be misled? In every contradiction to my earthly mind, I knew that following my Father's will was, and should always be, the only destination. No matter how hard I tried, my earthly mind could not arrive with any modal resolution.

Though just as to the reader of these words, there was so much depth to the story unfolding, I had to continue to remind myself how everything must appear to Lindsey. In the simplest terms, all that had occurred to her eyes was that she reached out to me, inviting me to church and the friendly conversations that ensued thereafter. Nothing had transpired beyond those situations save for the promise that she would meet up over the weekend. So through her eyes alone the gravity that waited ahead was really completely unknown. Was it possible that whatever circumstances drew her away from us meeting were caused by Lucifer intervening?

It was this reminder of the simplicity of the situation that helped ground my perspective in how our Father works when following His directive. Perhaps the idea of the fairytale ending unfolding was just adding anxiety that I had to learn how to handle. For to have faith is to trust in Him completely, including His timelines and His reasoning. All of the experiences leading into the day she was to receive the book had been a way for Him to test my soul, to stretch my faith to the limits. I could see that the potential for Love was held in His hand, and truly anything was possible at His will and His command. The recognition in His unyielding Love, brought forth a question in how a person should react to adversity along the spiritual journey. For when a person truly believes he is following a divine directive in the wake of multiple confirmations and answers through prayer, the continued action taken should be viewed as a demonstration of faith and the will to fulfill His calling. And if his understanding of our Father's words were incorrect, the continued pursuit of seeking guidance would lead to the necessary redirects. But the fine line that is crossed by many who follow this path is the line where the ego selectively hears His commands.

This selective hearing that has now been defined is the root of bias and how the Lord's will is twisted in a way flattering only to earthly eyes. This is the line where many who begin to hear our Father's voice choose to apply it in a way the mind thinks His voice should fit. To be honest, this is the reason for the many divisions across the globe and the fraternal orders that define religious homes. This does not mean that a person of zeal has not heard God's word, but rather has selectively chosen how to apply it and unconsciously chosen to halt along the journey's path at the hidden whisper of the ego. Those who are caught up in this lost place along the journey's path often are the ones telling the world the loudest how they have been found…and truly believe that they have. These are the ones who shout out their understanding with force to the lost. These are the zealous faithful who have actually seen truth while they are unknowingly lost.

But in understanding that all truth can be misguided when unconsciously shaped by the ego, it was important that I take the next steps with as much care as possible. In every action taken, I had always sought confirmation in pause. I never said, "This is what I am doing. Father, if I am wrong, let me know." To ask my Father a question demonstrated my desire to follow His will rather than follow my interpretation of something He possibly never said. And even when I thought I heard His answer once, I knew that I had to always ask again. His confirmations would come in twos, if I was to move to His command. The second question would require another method in the delivery of His answer. Seeking two confirmations was a way that a check-and-balance system was instilled within my spiritual education. Obsessive? Maybe. But it is necessary for the cause. This location on the path to the Promised Land had to be carefully and meticulously traversed.

This unyielding dedication to my Father in lieu of the worldly view could easily be misconstrued in definition through an earthly point-of-view. For a reader will see only this one side of the story and possibly attempt to apply an earthly bias to an interpretation unfolding. But over the next two days of prayer, my Father helped me see that it was only time and dedication to the labor of His Love that separated me from experiencing His fairytale kind of Love – with the hope that it could be experienced in Lindsey. It was in these days that He continued to guide me in direction, helping me see that it was only from my lens of perspective that Lindsey and I not yet meeting was something more than a blip on the Great Highway leading to Eternity.

Truly it must be comical to watch us from above; how one tiny speck of a moment in an infinite expanse of time can derail a person along the journey of learning to hear His Voice. But perhaps the greatest testament to this very test can be seen in those who have been written about in all of the days before us: the prophets of the Lord, the faithful who answered His call, the disciples, the leaders, those who pilgrimmed into the desert, and those who placed the blood of a Lamb over their doors. These are the faithful who ignored earthly interpretations and found faith in something greater than reason. So, too, would I find myself placed in a situation of stretching my

Crowns

mind beyond rational limitations. In the days to follow, I would demonstrate my faith – a faith that would go on to shape the course of Forever.

An Ark of Letters

How must it have seemed when Noah was tasked with building an ark? Endless days of labor were spent in building a vessel in spite of the ridicule others must have given him. God's promise to him of Forever was based on believing an idea that Noah had never even witnessed since water had never fallen from the sky. In the days of Noah, water originated from the ground. The idea that rain would fall from above was as foreign of an idea as telling someone in modern times that fire will one day burn inverted, where the flame and smoke are pulled below the surface – an impossible concept within the world that is known. The judgment which must have been placed on Noah somehow managed to survive the flood from those days and transcend generations. For when a person truly follows faith alone, people still pass judgment.

The irony in the way people judge others is how they will be found in the crosshairs of God's judgment. For the purpose is never to judge or speak about others. The purpose is to follow the path in finding our Father. Help. Hope. Love. These are the core tenets. If just a small fraction of the people on Earth could acknowledge this common ground and approach the world as a child learning to hear and see for the first time – everyday, for the rest of all time – Heaven on Earth would be revealed. But until the walls are broken down to following this ideal, it will remain hidden from earthly eyes.

So just as Noah was forced to follow an impossible task upon his journey in faith with our Father, so too would God's promise of Forever be the destination I sought through following His directives that I was given. And though I never doubted the promise – rather just questioned how to keep moving forward – I still had to understand how Gravity Calling was to be brought forth to Lindsey's attention. Was this the ending to be written and now it was an effort in getting it published? And if so, would the first time she would see the book only be once it was available to the public? Or perhaps there was a greater story to be written. Perhaps an even greater ending. I could not be certain, for I was still sorting out the meaning of the experience. I only knew that I had to forge onward without any doubt.

In prayer, my Father helped me understand that I was not to speak of or share any of my writing until a time of His choosing – that is except for the book to be delivered to Lindsey, which was still important for the journey. It still seemed there was much to be learned in running toward the destination of a Love to be found. During my prayers, I had continually been shared directives in building an ark. At first I thought any references to building an ark were not related to the Love story being written. And while it may sound a little crazy – I thought so too – it would turn out that building an ark for this Love story was part and parcel to seeing this portion of the journey through.

An Ark of Letters

After two days of prayer and ensuring I was taking the appropriate next steps forward, I devised a plan to build an ark for the book. It was an ark of letters, packed in white lace and blue, to be set upon the waters of the spirit and set sail into the great expanse of all His potential, as he willed my soul to do. Perhaps the whole effort would be for my soul alone, or perhaps it was for a story to transcend generations. The ark was a symbolic effort to bridge two souls found in a Divine language.

The evening of the second day, I went to the store and purchased all of the materials I would need to build the ark. And though I was no homemaker in artsy crafts, it was important that the vessel be labored over with a caring hand. On the third day, I had completed the task. I had crafted a box that would carry the book, packaged in the most symbolic ways. On the outside, the box was wrapped in baby blue tissue paper closest to its frame – symbolic to the blue cloth that covered the Ark of the Covenant in biblical days. On top of the blue tissue, the box was wrapped in white lace. The box was formed from a single-piece enclosure of cardboard with ratios that closely resembled both arks from biblical days. It may not have been perfect in dimensions, for I had to rely on the materials given. But it was a gesture that was intended to be read about and understood for upcoming generations as to the care that must permeate every effort of fulfilling Divine tasks upon the journey.

The interior of the box was filled with a pillowed padding of air, covered in off-white satin. The off-white color was used to demonstrate His purity through a vessel, though it would almost certainly have lost a portion of His perfection in transcendence. Or possibly the satin could be viewed as the color of "eggshell." And if the color was understood as such and not as "off-white," then it could be viewed as a shell housing life inside. For as a bird emerges into the world, the shell must be broken for life to be revealed. Inside of the box life would be resting upon the shell. And while there was no expectation that any of this effort would be understood to earthly eyes, it was intended in a conversation silent for the eyes of the soul to recognize.

At this point along the journey, I was still learning how to follow, though one day I would look back and understand the greater meaning of the efforts. But for now, the box appeared complete. Inside, the contents were placed in a way that would be perfect for her eyes to meet. Placed inside of the box was Lindsey's version of Gravity Calling, the coffee mug, and the bookmark. But most importantly, a letter was placed on top. The letter was housed in the same type of envelope trimmed in red as she would find in the safety deposit box in the days ahead. The letter included in the box housed the words of my soul, and a motion that would hopefully prompt her soul to move. It was an effort that had to occur since I would not be present, when she received the ark of letters packaged as a present.

The top of the box was folded over and closed. Outside of the box, a ribbon of lace was wrapped and tied in a bow. As an ode to the original intention of us meeting in a coffee shop

An Ark of Letters

as it had been written, the effort to deliver the ark would be symbolic to this effort. Since Lindsey was unable to meet my daughter and me at our chosen destination, the delivery of the ark would also demonstrate how the spirit works without movement. As Lindsey was at work on this third day, the ark was delivered to her office with Starbucks iced coffee, regular coffee served in bulk, cups, creamer, and all of the works. The coffee was intended to be placed in the break room and served for everyone in the office – a generally accepted practice and a gesture to lift everyone's spirits. The box would include a small card with Lindsey's name on it. Inside, the card would include a short one-liner about the coffee being delivered to her office for everyone since we were unable to meet at the coffee shop over the weekend.

When she opened the box, the letter that she would see in the envelope trimmed in red would house much more of my soul in written form than I initially expected to share. In the conversation that would have taken place over coffee, it would have been easy to dance around normal conversation while reminiscing of the past. In spoken conversation, this is the method in which everyone partakes. It is a craft that subconsciously occurs without the magnitude of being direct. But the words in the letter now served a different purpose. They were at the helm of the ark helping steer it to its destination.

The words that Lindsey would read that day, would place her significance in my life naked on a table, though not revealing all the book would share in any detail. It was important that she see the letter as the grandest potential or even none therein. For her it was only important that she know she was included in a book I had written. The "whys" and "what fors" would be for her to discover, if she chose to open the book and explore the words with her soul and heart. So just as it was important to share all of the written words included in the safety deposit box, without further adieu, here are the words of the letter included the ark.

...

Lindsey,

A little over three and a half years ago, our paths would cross for the first time here on Earth. It was a moment that I will never forget – a moment that I mentioned to you briefly when you reached out to me over the holidays. You never asked why I remembered the day so well, and I hoped that one day I would be able to share with you why that day was so engrained in my mind after all of these years. But, as everything would eventually come to play out, those words would have to come in the form of this letter instead of over a cup of coffee this past weekend.

It was during that time three and a half years ago, that I was experiencing one of the most difficult and darkest times of my life – though I masked it well from everyone around me. I was in the aftermath of a divorce and basically learning to live again. I am sure it was not too unlike everything you have been experiencing in the recent months – however I do understand no two situations are even partially the same. But that particular day our paths would cross, something special happened. While I was trying to paint the world in happiness in the midst of my pain, you painted mine that day. Your smile became my favorite smile. It inspired me, and I

An Ark of Letters

wrote about it. It led me home. That is the reason why I remember that day so vividly.

Years would pass, we'd stay in touch, and God would help my spiritual journey begin to take shape. I found myself writing a lot to help me understand everything happening to me on my journey. I eventually completed the book that is in the box with this letter. Writing this book is something that God tasked me to do, but it did not find the form you hold right now until I was called to go to Haiti. But all of that will make sense in short order. Most importantly, the reason it is important for you to receive this book now is because of what I said earlier about having written about the day we first met.

It is most important to me that you are the first person to read the words I wrote about you. No other eyes will have seen these words before you. All I ask is for you to turn to page 161, the chapter entitled "40 Days," and start reading from there. The beginning, for you, should be read after you've reached the end. In this box, you will find two more items. The first is a bookmark to mark your place along the way and the second is a locally handmade coffee mug. I figure if you are going to spend the time to read the words, you might as well be appropriately prepared for a late night reading session. Georgia also knows about everything and wanted to give you the mug this past weekend.

Always,
Jonathan

White Lace & Blue

There is an Old English rhyme that goes: "Something olde, something new, something borrowed, something blue, a sixpence in your shoe." The rhyme originated sometime around 1883 and has ever since been used in the context of weddings throughout the centuries. Though in the modern world, the final portion of the rhyme regarding a sixpence is mostly adhered to only in English traditions, the first four items in the rhyme are traditionally worn by a bride on her wedding day as a symbol of good luck and blessing.

While the rhyme carries a meaning much greater than the meaning most understand, traditionally the meanings of the four symbols a bride is to wear are as follows: An item that is worn by the bride to represent "something old" is intended to be a symbol of "her family, her past, and traditions." "Something new" is meant to carry the meaning of "the future and all that awaits." The item that is borrowed, is intended to represent "borrowed happiness." Often, the borrowed item is received from another bride that has come before her, in a symbolic tradition of passing on borrowed happiness – a form of bridal lineage. The color blue as it is to be worn in a wedding is symbolic to Love, purity, and fidelity. In Christian weddings, the color blue is also meant to represent the Virgin Mary.

The symbolism a bride is meant to demonstrate in the actions taken during a wedding is perhaps the closest example to the actions I had taken in crafting an ark to carry the book to its destination. Every ounce of care that could be poured into the effort was of utmost importance in making sure my soul was carried through the distance separating Lindsey and me in earthly forms, for this place on the journey required the spirit to move as my feet remained in the sand. Some may think that investing so much effort into such symbolism is a waste of energy for what amounts to superstition, but what is missed in this interpretation is that the Spirit is living and moves within everything. Every action taken should always demonstrate every ounce of knowledge and truth in pursuing the destination. Symbolism, by definition, is the recognition of another person's efforts in demonstration of something greater. But to the person evoking symbolic efforts, they should not be performed in empty gestures. The efforts in every action taken should hold truth filled with the spirit, not symbolism of broken understanding. The same can be said for a bride. The truth in "the old, the new, something borrowed, and something blue" should be demonstrated with radiant understanding of the gravity of the actions taken, though that is rarely the case.

Whether or not a bride understands the true importance of the symbolism in the items is never really questioned. Most often brides only want to make sure they do not welcome any undue superstition. And perhaps the pretense to this particular effort made is actually one of the greatest reasons marriage has become such a failure in this age. The very understanding of the spiritual steps taken is often overlooked for the idea of earthly Love, earthly safety, and earthly security. But the true reason a bride is tasked with making such symbolic efforts through the items worn on her wedding day is to demonstrate her understanding of how God is embodied in every thread worn, in every thread of Love formed. The symbolism of old and new should be seen in a similar light to baptism through the washing away of the past for the commitment to a Love greater than earthly explanation. A wedding is the embodiment of Ever-After and should be seen with same strength and gravity of a spiritual commitment to our Father.

Though I would not see the symbolic nature of the Ark of Letter's adornments to the materials and colors that are the foundation of a wedding ceremony, it is a wondrous example of how our Father works – a sight that can only be witnessed in hindsight after further growth. To my soul, the Ark of Letters was crafted in the perfect embodiment of my intention and my actions. My soul was moving freely in a waltz with the spirit as my mind only brought to form the expression of their movements. It was a demonstration of my soul threaded in the hues and materials of white lace and blue – the very same colors and materials a bride is to wear on the day she proclaims to Love, "I do."

In hindsight I can now see that the choice of white materials for the Ark of Letters embodied the same materials of a

Crowns

wedding dress. The lace adorned the outside of the box, just as the lace of wedding dress is what is noticed at first blush. The satin material of the pillow inside was where the meaning of the colors of off-white and eggshell collided. But the choice of satin was a curious choice. At the time it represented the material of a soft pillow-top. In retrospect, the satin was the perfect compliment to the lace, as they are both the chief components of a wedding dress. But at the time the ark was crafted, I only saw white and blue. The white held the grandest meaning – so much color, so much hue.

As the ark was crafted, I began to understand that, perhaps, the most perfect color able to be viewed by the human eyes was not a color at all, but rather every color wrapped up in One. It is often a color taken for granted, for it arrives without a splash of emotion in its purest form. It is the color of true beauty. It is the color of perfection. It is the color of unity divine. It is the color white. When most people view the color palette, the color white tends to be cast aside as not even a color, though it is often placed alongside the other colors in the palette. It is an enigma wrapped up in undefined representation, but the irony is it contains every color in a single presentation.

Tennessee white is the most spectacular white I have witnessed. It is a white that is composed of a chemistry of country, delicacy, and femininity. The very thought of Tennessee white invokes thoughts of the green rolling hills, tanned leather, and the frills of lace. At the thought of the color, I see the Tennessee sun reflecting rays of light from its surface, indiscernible to

White Lace & Blue

most everyone without sight of the spirit. It is a white that can only be embodied in the material of lace in order to paint the imagery of Southern charm, blonde hair, Tennessee sun, and moonlight-reflecting lakes. Tennessee white is a color that can only be seen, when the spiritual aspects of Tennessee are present in its sheen. It is a description that may cause some to scratch their heads, but it is a color the eyes see and the feeling of how the soul is led.

When I see Tennessee white presented in the form of lace, I see the geometric patterns of perfection – a mandala of the Lord's breath. In another location, white lace would not carry the same meaning, though perhaps it could be just as grandiose in another way to me. But in the presence of those in Tennessee, it was the definition of a spiritual waltz in certainty. This is the feeling my soul experienced when choosing the color and pattern to be included on the outside of the Ark of Letters. But if the ark was only crafted in white, it would appear too wedding-like. Instead, the white lace had to be wrapped around the color blue, to offset any preconceived notions. And while I have already brought to light part of the meaning for the choice of baby-blue as the color underlying, it is also important to share how this very color requires white in its creation. Typically the color white is used to soften and lighten other colors. A bold blue may become a cerulean or baby-blue with a touch of it added. Midnight red will become pink – a color that will be revealed in Book III for its spiritual importance. The other colors become shades of pastel – the colors of Easter; the colors of spiritual zeal.

Crowns

Most people would agree that with age comes wisdom, but maybe it is best understood as a return to spiritual recognition. However, the reasons and rationale in the meaning of colors is often best understood by a child without worldly notions. For as a child begins to understand the world around him, spiritual concepts spill forth unnoticed. It is only through the eyes of the soul that a child's eyes of wonder reveal a truth untold. When I was a child, I exhibited this very same spiritual recognition, as did my cousin Bryan. There was a conversation we had as young children that we still talk about to this day, where we spoke of recognized spiritual truths housed in a specific color and shape.

"What is your favorite color, Jonathan?" Bryan's voice echoed out from the room next to the room I was in. We were both children at the time. I was maybe around seven or eight years old which would put Bryan around the age of twelve or thirteen.

"The blue square." I replied.

Without missing a beat, Bryan said, "Good. That is what I thought."

No other questions were asked as we went about playing as children do. It is times like these that most children would never give the question asked – or the answer given – a second thought. It is a time that seems hopelessly lost in the banter between two children at play. But the exchange that took place that day between my cousin Bryan and me would be the first spiritual dialogue that was exchanged between our two souls in the earliest days of youth.

The dialogue stuck with us for ages. Perhaps it was the seemingly random answer to an oddly timed question. Perhaps it was Bryan's nonchalant retort to my own answer. Whatever the case may be that caused that particular conversation to stick with us through our years, there was an unquestionable resonance that held song with each of our souls. It was as if the words were packaged up in a delicate wrapping to be opened up at a point much later in our lives that God had chosen far before we saw His plan unfolding. It was a moment of splendor shared between two children. The very idea that a favorite color included a shape in the response may have been dismissed as mindless gibberish to others listening, but to Bryan and me, it served as a moment of confirmation.

I have to believe that long before we were ever born onto this Earth, we were children in Heaven staring down at this little blue marble called Earth. In the heavens, we understood our bond as brothers. For reasons that were unclear at this point in the journey, there came a time that we each departed the heavens for Earth to be born unto our families knowing that one day we would discover our origin and purpose. Perhaps all of the people in our earthly families carry the same bond of having known one another in the heavens long before we ever arrived on Earth. Perhaps it was part of the divine plan all along. Perhaps the reasons are more specific to a divine lineage. After all, that was one of the questions I asked Bryan during that first phone call that started this journey. It was a divinely planned day all along, one chosen by His hand. November 25, 2011, was the day God spoke so divinely to each of us in response to a simple question, and perhaps lineage was somehow part of this response as well.

The question and response that Bryan and I shared that day was one that seemed planned from before we stepped foot on Earth. Perhaps it was just a spiritual recognition of two souls speaking underneath the banter of mindless conversations. But, I like to think that the question and answer we shared that day was similar to the type of question and answer that is often joked about within the scientific community regarding time machines. There is a philosophical concept that if a time machine is invented in the future then the present moment could be experienced as the past. This would mean that man could theoretically be visited by a future version of themselves from the future. While the idea is more of a fun and hypothetical thought, the humor is in the solution scientists and philosophers alike decided would the best way to test and validate this possibility. Since the idea was quite perplexing, someone suggested that every person should have a question and response that a "future self" could ask their "present self" wherein only the present and future versions would know the answer. Whoever it was that first originated this idea may have done so out of humor, but it has managed to seep its way into television and movie scripts throughout the decades. The comments may be passed off as quick one-liners, but they exist nonetheless. But the idea of having a question that only your present self would know the answer to is similar to how I view the question and response Bryan and I shared that day. For there is no reason that such a question about colors would warrant a response of a shape until the spiritual context is explored.

Over the course of the journey, both Bryan and I have learned so much regarding colors, shapes, and how the universe is architected. While it may seem like a very elementary topic to address on Earth, in a spiritual context it is quite the opposite. Most of Book VIII is dedicated to explaining colors, shapes, numbers, archetypes, and how they are all part of the fabric to All That Is. In brevity, though, it would be very difficult to address here. But just in exploring the spiritual meaning of the color of blue, it should be seen as the color of the Spirit (like an endless body of water) and identified as representative of Heaven. But to bring this reasoning into perspective, it is also important to have another color in which to compare. The color red should be understood as the color of Love, passion, and identified with Earth. When red and blue are mixed, purple is formed – the color used in almost all religions to represent royalty. Purple is the perfect union of the heavenly-lead soul and the concept of Love that must be learned upon the Earth. Betwixt the two, the concept of royalty is born – a perfect Love, not of earthly origin, but of Heavenly design experienced upon the Earth. This is the Love this book is about; a Love that transcends Heaven and Earth and binds souls across the Great Expanse.

And while I will not belabor the topics of Book VIII here, it is important to understand at a very high level why the choice of "square" was used in my response to Bryan. It should be seen that spheres are shapes of perfection, with no points and no ends. A sphere is the shape of the foundation, before creation came to be. Squares are an earthly creation of arbitrary points that must have ends to exist in the world in which we live. And while the truth in how a square is formed goes much further than the connection of four lines, let's just say it takes eight interlocking spheres to form a ninth sphere within, bound by a box that is viewed from straight above to earthly eyes as a square. It is okay if that description garners pause. It is okay to shake your head and save the exploration of that idea for another day. For now, it should just be seen that a square is to the color red, just as a sphere is to the color blue. In this, it can be understand how the response of "blue square" as my favorite color, demonstrated not just the idea of Heaven above, but how Heaven and Earth are One. It was almost as if I could have answered "purple" in response, but that answer would have only been heard in earthly words. Instead, the response given was the only possible way for two souls to say, "I see you," as they were both learning to see.

There may be some "whats?!" and "huhs?!" to the previous explanation, but it is important that the response was included here in this section. For this portion of the story in Book II tells a greater story that will continue to be revealed after returning to it from the completion of the nine book journey. In fact, all of the books will continue to reveal layers upon layers to His Story – each time revealing more and more of His Glory. Simple acts of spiritual demonstration embody layers of meaning. Just the example of the act of giving the Ark of Letters may, at first, only be truly understood at the surface.

But through the study of the colors and the architecture to the Earth, the depths of how the Spirit moves begins to be revealed. All of these Books of Nine exhibit the same facets of layered understanding, though some may scrutinize and judge each layer based on their own journey's limits. However, it is important to understand that every road leads back home, and some are here to share His Story in a way to help guide the other souls. Few will ask for guidance. Fewer will accept the response. Even fewer still will seek truth by removing the chains bound by ego's locks. But in the story to be told, it will always be one of Love. For this is His Story, His Proclamation. This is the journey Home.

Home

Not many feelings top the feeling of "home" – the feeling of knowing that all of the surroundings are familiar, personal, and filled with Love. The latter part of the description may not be the first thought that comes to mind, but it is the very essence of Home. Think of Thanksgiving dinners, and Christmas get-togethers. Think of coming home to a spouse who meets you at the door. Think of a dog that runs to greet you or a cat's simple meow. Think of children running in the backyard or up and down apartment stairs. Perhaps it is the ride in the elevator from the ground to where you live. But maybe the greatest recognition in the feeling of Home cannot be felt until it is gone.

Think of a long trip away from home – maybe a vacation to paradise that is said to be like Heaven on Earth. A person can experience the wonders of the Earth and Love every minute. But whether it occurs on the plane ride back, or walking through the front door, the feeling of Home calling a person back cannot be ignored. It is the place that "essence" may be the best explanation of the ineffable feeling which is embodied in how a person returns to his beginning. It should be seen in a similar fashion to an origin story unfolding, or the building blocks of lineage. It is the essence that gives way to the definition of heritage.

Sometimes a person "just knows" a location is where they are meant to be. Sometimes a location is never questioned, it just always was and always will be. It is a tug across the cosmos on the heartstrings of the soul, drawing a person near to a place he can call Home. It is said that "home is where the heart is" but this just an earthly interpretation, for "Home is where the soul is" when it has returned to its beginning. For it should be understood that the essence of Home that permeates through earthly locations is the place where the soul sees glimmers of recognition in a location that cannot be seen with earthly eyes, only experienced through the veil that divides.

The first time my soul found the comfort of Heaven was a feeling so remarkable that a description cannot be written. Once this feeling had been brought to my earthly awareness, everything else I experienced paled in comparison. It would take quite some time to begin to understand just how this feeling of our soul's Home permeates through existence. The removal of earthly sight and suppression of the ego, were the main contributors to the prohibition of the Spirit. Once the barrier began to be broken down, the essence of Heaven beamed through the crumbling divide like rays of light pouring through cracks and holes of a crumbling stone wall. The glimmers of Home ignited my soul with its warmth. It was Spring's return from Winter's cold and gloomy hold.

This return of Spring could be seen along my journey as the way this Love story was unfolding. Through my spiritual

Home

eyes I saw glimmers of hope, to the warmth of His Light through a spiritual Love and walk in the Light. This Love was experienced through the Love story with Lindsey, just as life is witnessed sprouting forth in the spring. The blossoming seeds and sprouts of greenery are the hope that is given that life will return from Winter's life-suppressing thievery. The anticipation to the release of Winter's grasp was the feeling of the gravitational pull of Home's essence. For me, the story of how it would all unfold with the Ark of Letters delivered to Lindsey was not even a potential, it was a certainty.

I saw a Love story unfolding, though it defied all earthly logic. The obstacles placed before me were enough to derail most souls on the journey. It is true the obstacles could be viewed as potential warnings and signs to an unfavorable ending to the story. Instead, with each obstacle I faced, I sought guidance to understand whether to stop or proceed. This single question to my Father may have made the biggest difference along the journey, for it demonstrated acceptance of His will and removal of my ego. Though it should be understood that this portion of the journey was still a place of learning for me, these were the days I sought to understand every lesson in His teachings.

To many who see obstacles in life, the ego takes hold and says, "I've got this" and steers the mind. Some will drive through the obstacles headstrong, oblivious to the warning signs before them. Others will allow the ego to rationalize "turning around," "taking a different path," or "avoiding it all together." But the way the spirit works is always in the humbled submission to the will of our Father. The best action to take is never ego's rationale. Instead, the lesson is always learning to hear His voice – seeking guidance through Him and acceptance of His choice.

For me, in the delivery of the Ark of Letters, I was exposed in a way that was most uncomfortable. Through earthly eyes I saw the effort as she would see it. I saw how it would come out of left-field. I saw every reason to have walked away. I saw every obstacle as a way to change directions and take a different path instead. But I also saw hope, and the potential for her Amazing, though my mind rationalized only the slightest chance of Love's survival through the written pages.

But in a spiritual sense, I was a proud child. I was a student that had sought the Teacher's guidance. I asked for help. I asked for His direction. I asked how it should be done and what actions would please Him. I asked for guidance in handling the obstacles. I asked for His hand to help me through the most difficult ones. I asked for special tutoring away from the eyes of everyone. I asked for everything possible I could think of to demonstrate my reliance on Him rather than the ego. Through this humbled series of questions and the responses I had received, I felt peace in my walk – peace the Ark would be well received..

On the third day after Lindsey and I were to meet, the Ark was delivered to her office, along with the letter and Starbucks coffee. After it was dropped off, I went to a soccer field where I frequently find solitude and pray. It is a field that sits between three churches in Brentwood, Tennessee, just off of the interstate. It was here that I continued to pray, I sought guidance and searched for calm in the midst of my anxiety. Through every action taken (as my journals will show), I fought battles with the ego. To follow His will and extinguish earthly rationale, was quite possibly the hardest battle I ever had to face along the journey. It was the only place that the spiritual walk had bubbled to the surface in a way for others – especially Lindsey – to take notice. As I prayed, I sought further help. And though my Father's response was brief, I want to include the journal entry that was written down, just after it occurred.

...

March 18, 2014

As I prayed and meditated after lunch, I had one more brief experience in the heavens. My prayer was about finding clarity in the finality of my job. I heard God's call, but was hoping to understand how I needed to transition smoothly. I also prayed that my actions with giving my book to Lindsey were just. I felt spiritually confident they were, but I felt that I would probably be left in a gap where I would not know for a while if I took the correct spiritual action. I felt that I did, but obviously this is the single biggest thing that has happened to me in a spiritual sense – so I have some fragility to the outcome.

My experience in the heavens was without form in vision, but I was present in spirit. I knew I was in the presence of other angels as well, though I could not see them. Suddenly, I heard a male voice – God's voice – that echoed throughout the heavens. He said, "Go home." I immediately returned to my body.

Crowns

My first thought was in the literal – "Should I go to my apartment? Is something wrong?" But I immediately stomped that thought out. I knew it was of spiritual nature, so it only took a few seconds to find spiritual recognition in the words. It was God telling me to "Go. Fall in Love with Lindsey." He was answering my question as to how I would know if I took the correct spiritual action with delivering the book to her. At first blush, most people would wonder how I arrived at "going home" meant "falling in Love with Lindsey" but that is part of the story in my book. The Promised Land is the destination of Love in another – the place that God led the tribes standing in the desert in Deuteronomy. This was the place they were to grow and prosper – all provided by God's hand.

I also had made another analogy to "home" in my book – this one written well before my understanding of the spiritual journey being tantamount to the journey through the first five books of the Bible. The analogy I wrote about in my book about Love is, "If falling in Love is the leap, knowing you are in Love is pulling the parachute and just the glide home." I also recently felt inspired to write a maxim that I have not placed on Twitter or anywhere else yet, but it also used the destination of home as a metaphor to Love. The maxim goes, "Home is where the soul finds its counterpoint in another; it is not a specific location or place to be. We all long to be home." So, to sum up this experience – in response to my prayer, God told me, "Go. You have my blessing of Love with Lindsey."

...

The response was a demonstration of how His communication works. The reference to Home was onion-layered, holding so many meanings in just two simple words. And while at first I would understand many of the layers housed within, it would not be until nearly a year later that I would

Home

catch the most obvious meaning. At the time I understood how the reference to Home was intertwined so deeply with the story and all that had been experienced and written. And though I sought guidance before taking any actions, I saw His confirmation in all of the actions taken. During this time I expected Gravity Calling to be the only book written. It seemed like the book was the journey with the outcome as the destination.

However, as it must be obvious in this book's reading, the journey included much more to be written. This book, in particular, was the very last on the nine completed – for the journey had to be traversed, to reveal the first book's true meaning. The efforts taken, and the response given by my Father that third day, laid the groundwork to the greatest Love Story of modern days. On the third day the ark housing my soul set sail into the unknown, I held onto hope it was the vessel that would carry me Home. This third day, I would come to understand, held so many symbolic meanings, but at this point I was blind to that aspect of the symbolism.

The third day should be seen as metaphorical to the death and resurrection of Christ. It was on the third day after Christ's crucifixion that a mortal form was given Spiritual Life. It was a story of Ever-After told for generations, shared in a way with layers of meaning. For just as the third day revealed His Divine Truth in Christ, this portion of the journey held a symbolic version of His Truth in my life. On the day Lindsey and I were to meet so I could give her the book, my body was symbolically crucified at the coffee shop. It was the day I

Crowns

would look back and see as the time I chose God over earthly rationale. For when the Ark of Letters, wrapped up in white lace and blue set sail in the destination of Love, it truly was His Will – His Voice – calling my soul Home.

God Works In Twos

Nothing ceases to surprise me anymore. The way that God works in our lives is miraculous unto its own, but to see the Spirit in action, living, breathing, in a way that transcends a fairytale into a real and tangible story, is a miracle in every way. That is just how it has been over the two and a half years of the journey. Day in and day out, there was always a miracle to witness. Sometimes it was something simple, something small. Sometimes it was just a text message or a simple phone call. Sometimes it was as grandiose as my soul being taken to the heavens or the angels appearing on Earth to me. Sometimes it was the Voice of God. Sometimes it was His divine symbols. From the days of finding a wad of cash on my doorstep following a conversation I had with Bryan, to praying for help in my career and having three jobs fall in my lap – everyday housed something special.

Gravity Calling embodied the moments I would learn to hear His voice through the world around me. It was a time when a thought of bringing light to Lindsey meant a morning of scrambling around the greater Nashville area seeking homemade chocolates to deliver anonymously…complete with every obstacle possible. The obstacles nearly made me stop, nearly made me quit. The obstacles seemed like blatant warnings to halt on the path that I was following. But each time I would pray for help and express this frustration and thoughts of giving up, God would inexplicably offer His hand if I was willing to take hold. He would lead me through troubled waters. He would lead me in an ascent. He would lead me through the desert on the way to the Promised Land.

I found myself standing with my feet in the sand, staring at what I could only believe was the image of the Promised Land. It was a destination of Love, a destination of Hope. But most importantly, it was a destination of Trust; trust in a Father that was holding me all along. I was a child learning to walk, learning to run. I was a child who needed the help of my Father and the confidence that He imparted. It was the strength in His voice that kept me going strong. It was the Voice in His strength that was guiding me Home.

Every time I was ready to give up, He always seemingly had something to say about it. But regardless of the situation and the circumstances presented, His resolve always ended with Him saying, "Just hang on, Son. I promise there is more. Trust Me. It may not make sense, but that is what this part is about. Follow My lead. I promise I'll hold you all of the way Home." At times it was unfathomable. At times I questioned my very own sanity. There is no doubt that my journals from this time will echo that very same sentiment. There were days that I was filled with so much frustration at not understanding all of His reasoning that I would scream out or find myself crying for much longer than I care to admit. It was a rollercoaster I boarded when I prayed that night in November and said,

God Works In Twos

"Help me. I cannot do this alone. I know there is more. I know you are in control – not me. I never was. I see that now. Father show me, and I will follow....I will follow unconditionally." And I did.

The unconditional commitment meant chasing down chocolate in spite of common sense. The commitment led me to building an Ark of Letters and sending it on its way with my soul encased within, hoping it found the destination of Love, through all of my trust in Him. It was a moment that defied logic and all earthly reasoning. But there it was, sailing off into the distance. Everything it was sailing into was uncharted territory – at least that is how it appeared to me. My prayers on the eighteenth of March were answered back with unconditional Love wrapped up in certain uncertainty. Two words separated Love and Eternity. Those words were "Go Home." I was certain the destination was as He intended it to be and certain the actions were just. However, I was uncertain of all that remained ahead, which was the hardest part of unconditional trust.

How must have it have felt for Noah to ride out the flood, only to have the first bird he sent out never return? It would take a second dove sent out upon the waters to return with a branch – a twig from a tree – that must have given Noah a resounding sigh of relief. There he was, having followed an unthinkable journey to find himself and his family vulnerable upon the waters. Everything had defied earthly rationale, only to be bobbing up and down in the waters, finding continued faith that God would prevail. Everything to that point for Noah was so divinely orchestrated, but the mind is a funny thing. In spite of all of the miracles performed through God's hand, the ego can create doubt and justify nearly anything. The seven days that separated the two doves that Noah sent out must have been a grand testimony of his strength and his faith. There he was with no reason to doubt, but with no land in sight and a dove that never returned.

The second dove that was sent out was a symbol that has been shared for generations. It was a sign that Noah had not given up, and a time when God replied to his faithful. It was one of the earliest symbols of how God works in twos. There are examples of two birds recurring throughout Biblical stories – the sign of God's workings. There are signs and wonders that are witnessed or performed in twos. In Gravity Calling much of the reasoning in the requirement of how God speaks through two people was discussed in how Bryan and I had embarked on the journey together. And quite honestly, until we had our shared experience in the heavens during the first few months into the journey, it was still easy to rationalize it was all created in the mind and not of His Glory. Until that point, it was possible that every divine example signed by God's hand was only hope impersonating His signature through the mind of man.

To have two people experience the same story – perhaps through different lenses or vantage points – is a way He alleviates any doubt that His demonstrations are nothing short of His design. The requirement of two points is what forms a line, and gives an earthly construct to an impossibly-perfect

God Works In Twos

architecture of the Divine. The two points used to form a line should be seen as the root of any example as to why it takes two, to see through spiritual eyes. This is the reason that two symbols and signs for each of God's actions are manifest in so many Biblical stories. It is why there must be two witnesses who will prepare the way for the return of the Messiah. It takes two. It always has. It always will.

It was on the evening after having sent out the Ark of Letters upon the Waters of the Spirit, that I spoke with Bryan on the phone. We had not spoken much over the previous months, but I was exasperated – spiritually exhausted – and needed to hear the comfort of my brother's words. When we spoke, I would not be let down. He was really excited to tell me about a special moment that happened to him and his fiancée, Mindi. At the time, he knew nothing about the Ark, and very little about Lindsey. All that he had to share was in no way intended to have any parallels to the walk I was experiencing. To his spiritual eyes, the story he wanted to share was purely about him and Mindi.

Bryan went on to tell me how Mindi had received a package in the mail earlier that day. It arrived unannounced, with no fanfare, with no explanation. Inside of the box was a Bible and a letter from a person she had not spoken to in years. The letter told a story of how Mindi had been on the mind of that old friend for reasons that even her friend did not know. All that was apparent was that this friend was led on a mission, to deliver a Bible with Mindi's name imprinted upon it. The letter went on to say that it would be great for them to catch up again some time, but the reason for the package was only for the Bible this time. With little else to go on and no other reason given, Mindi shared the letter with Bryan, who in turn shared it with me.

When I heard the story, my eyes welled up with tears. I could not help but see all of the symbolism delivered from this person's actions and what it meant both to Bryan and to me. To Bryan, the heaviest weight upon his shoulders had been how to tell Mindi all about our experiences. He knew bridging the idea that he travels to the heavens and speaks to angels was a topic that could be poorly received, though Mindi carried a strong spirituality. Part of the journey Bryan and I had come to understand was the importance of a spouse who carried an unbridled Love in our Father and was open to speaking about it. The importance placed upon this area was the greatest burden carried by him because he knew how much God had led them together, but he feared Mindi's reaction. Though he attempted several times to approach the topic head-on, it was never well received, so he continued to regroup in his approach. But this time he could use the receipt of the Bible as an example of how God was working in their lives – all without having to give examples that could be difficult to accept for anyone's mind.

We spoke for quite a while about all of the potential carried through this action. To the person who sent the Bible, she blindly answered a divine call to action – a call which would push an entire line of dominos into motion in response to her effort. It was the kind of moment that makes a person smile

God Works In Twos

when he sees how a complex, curving line of dominoes can be set into motion with just one light touch of a finger in the briefest of moments. Sometimes the touch is accidental. Sometimes it is unexpected. But when the line of dominoes has been set up, that light touch is all it takes to start the motion. This is how the Spirit moves within us. Every person is connected to a line of dominoes unaware to where any of the paths lead. Sometimes all it takes is the nudge from another to send all of the spiritual dominoes into motion around us, revealing the divinity in following His lead.

Bryan used the example to open up more to Mindi, though I will leave that side of the story for him to share when he is ready. But the importance in the catalyst of Mindi's friend's action is one that cannot be overstated. For just as the action of sending the Bible held so much meaning to Bryan, it also held meaning specifically for Mindi. It was received at a time in her life, during a specific series of events, in a way that could not have had a more pronounced signature to the architecture of His Divinity.

And while the two of them were able to experience such a divine moment in their lives, there was one more divine aspect viewed from the perspective of my spiritual eyes. For just as I had, earlier in the day, sent the Ark of Letters upon the Spirit of the Waters, I would be able to witness the very same action performed for Bryan and Mindi to see. The receipt of a Bible could not have been any more symbolic to the actions I had taken earlier in the day. My soul was wrapped up in the words of Gravity Calling, packaged in a box for Lindsey to receive.

Crowns

Inside of the box she would find a letter – arriving without fanfare or expectation – sharing similar sentiments to the letter Mindi received.

Though the comparison should not be mistaken in saying the words Lindsey received carried the same meaning as the words received by Mindi, the effort should be understood for the symbolism involved and His artful display in foreshadowing this story's ending. It was more akin to my Father saying to me, "Son, Gravity Calling is your Love story. This one is mine. The two are One, though divided over time. The actions you have taken have been performed in the same response to the Spirit as in the example of the receipt of the Bible you just witnessed. Have faith in Me. Trust in your actions. For there is an even greater story being written. It will take some time to see, but this is not just your story with Lindsey; this is the story of you and Me. Sit tight. Hold on. There will be some bumps along the road. But trust me, the road is more of an ascent – and the bumps, well, that is just turbulence."

First Day of Spring

In 2015, a year after Gravity Calling was completed, the first day of Spring was ushered in with a mammoth amount of spiritual symbolism. Though the journey I had embarked upon in November, 2011, would continue to unveil layers of meaning well after the immediate time being, it was the first day of Spring that truly caught my eye. It was a day that made me stop and realize how all of the experiences on the journey had occurred on dates that would hold future relevance and meaning.

In 2015, the first day of Spring arrived with a full moon – a supermoon – for all of the world to see. The term "supermoon" is not a fancy term or marketing word. Rather it is the description of the moon as it reaches perigee – a point in the moon's elliptical orbit that draws the moon closer to Earth than other points of the orbit. At perigee, the moon appears slightly larger to the naked eye due to its astronomical closeness compared to its location on most other nights. But it is not just the point of perigee that makes the moon "super." It also must occur on the day of the twenty-eight day cycle when the moon is at its fullest. With the two points of the moon's cycle occurring on the same day, the moon appears larger and brighter than any other time to the naked eye.

Crowns

For the supermoon to occur on a vernal equinox is a rare occurrence indeed. The vernal equinox is the point in the Earth's cycle when the sun is directly in line with the equator – the first day of Spring. It is the point when the length of the day starts to shift to longer times as the Earth tilts more favorably toward the sun. And while the Northern hemisphere on Earth would experience this combination of phenomena, another celestial event was set to occur. On the very first day of Spring over the North Pole region of the Earth, the world would experience a total eclipse of the sun.

Solar eclipses are rare, but this one would hold even grater rarity in its manifestation, for this eclipse occurred directly over the North Pole region. And while there is much symbolism that can be explored, the importance for now is in the rarity of the event and the combination of its occurrence on the day of the vernal equinox and supermoon. Some may question the importance of celestial events as many religions teach their followers not to turn to signs in the sky for events to come, but the irony is that celestial events are divine markers placed by the hand of God. They are ways for the perceptive to understand His intentions through the study of religion. But it is the line crossed when people only study the sky in lieu of following God that the warnings are intended to prevent.

The importance of these celestial events of the sun and the moon in the year of 2015 should not be cast aside. For on the dates of four successive feasts of the Lord occurring on the Judaic calendar in 2014 and 2015, the moon experiences another anomaly. On these days of feast the moon turns blood red for a small portion of time – a celestial event caused when the moon is cast in the Earth's shadow. The occurrence of a "blood moon" is another rarity, but to have four blood moons fall in series on Jewish days of feast should be viewed as an intersect of divinity. And while it is not the intention to bring focus to a specific theory that has arisen in modern times, it is important to see it as "another one of His signs." For the combination of the blood moons on Jewish holidays, coupled with the supermoon and solar eclipse over the north pole on the first day of Spring, is a series of events that will not be seen again for hundreds of thousands of years – well past mankind's cycles of generations.

The series of events that occurred on the first day of Spring in 2015, should be seen as just another piece of His Story. A year prior – in the context of this book – 2014 held just as much symbolism to me in my walk. It was just a few days prior to the first day of Spring that Lindsey's book was delivered to her. From that day forward, it was a time of internal tribulation, as I sought to find peace through prayer for the actions taken. I prayed that I would be shown clarity in the next steps of the journey, and to maintain strength in the efforts I was tasked to take with delivering the book to Lindsey. I sought peace in knowing that the dates of March 28th – 30th for the trip to Ponte Vedra were the dates He intended – and that there was enough time for Lindsey to read the book, find the key, and open the box that would lead her there.

It was also during this time that I was personally being led to Florida. Again, there was internal tribulation as to how this would all unfold. It was evident that my Father was providing for me during all of the steps of the journey, but I still struggled in earthly rationale to see His works as He intended for me to see them. When I had returned from Haiti, I had three messages about job offers but no further direction. And while I saw the potential in all of them and entertained pursuing them all simultaneously, I really had no idea how it would all play out. All I knew was that, against all earthly rationale, my Father had provided everything along the way and I knew He would continue to do so at this point as well.

If the supermoon and total eclipse of the sun in 2015 could be viewed as symbolic to everything I was to experience one year before, then it could be seen that the events that unfolded that day in 2014 were tantamount to the immaculate demonstration of the hand of the Lord. I used to think that acceptance of God was enough. It seemed like action meant everything – the fairytale ending to this walk upon the Earth. But then I realized, acceptance was not enough. It was the journey forward that was required to demonstrate faith in the walk. It was somewhere during the course of the journey that even this demonstration began to become blurred, as I began to be shown how to see through the divide of Heaven and Earth. The spiritual eyes that were hidden from light for the first thirty years of my life were starting to see shapes and see form. But rather than extrapolate any further on all that I was learning, perhaps it is best for the reader to see the journey as I saw it unfolding. For though it will be seen that there was still so much more that would be revealed to me in the days and

First Day of Spring

years to come, at the time of the ark having set sail, I was just looking for a branch held in the beak a dove. The following is my journal entry from the first day of Spring in 2014 – a day my soul found perigee to the face of the Lord; a day that my spiritual eyes blinked to the brightness of the sun.

...

March 20, 2014

Today I received three written and signed job offers on the exact same day. I had been praying for guidance on my next steps, and God had told me He would provide. I had faith, and in so, I saw His will multiplied around me. Deuteronomy 28:7 was a verse given to me by Wilson when we met to review his offer. This was confirmation of the plans I have on the 28th with Lindsey. That particular verse ends with a reference to the number seven.

I said a prayer before going to sleep last night after the conversation with Bryan yesterday. The prayer had to do with whether everyone is a projection of one's own self. It was akin to asking if everyone exists as one. Bryan kept repeating "spoiler alert" in our conversation which made me begin to piece together the concept of everyone as one. "Spoiler alert" is something that Lindsey said to me in the very first conversation we had. No one else around me has used that term, but Bryan felt inclined to use it repeatedly in our conversation. Seeing this little nuance brought forth the manifestation of my prayer on Earth. It is a concept as old as time, but cannot be understood until you can actually see the spirit in another through spiritual eyes.

Today at lunch, Bryan called with a projection of seeing his reflection reaching through a mirror and wrestling with it. I disambiguated it with

Crowns

the prayer from the night before and explanation of Love being the definition of two becoming one – which means that everyone and everything should be seen as one, bound by a universal Love. Love in another is the definition of the hand reaching through the mirror. Conversations continued throughout the day and evening. He sent tons of texts my way. The seventh text from him indicated that the angels disambiguated the numbers fifteen and twenty-two from an experience I had a few days ago. He was told that the numbers were pointers to The Book of Thomas (a Gnostic text). As it turns out, verse seventy-seven is pretty special too. The book of Thomas is the key to the Bible. It is the answer to all of the questions that cause contradictions. If the Bible is a cypher of sorts, the Book of Thomas is the Codex. The numbers fifteen and twenty-two came up in conversation because Bryan started using Samson as an example in conversation. I told him about my experience and how I was led to research the book of Judges from the earlier experience. We realized that each of those pointers were keys to our conversation, which eventually led him to Thomas.

This evening I prayed asking God to take a piece of me and give it to Jason and help him find Him. I also prayed to take a piece of me and give it to Lindsey and help her find strength. I also offered my ultimate sacrifice to show Him I acknowledged His will – which was to demonstrate that He could take my life and help Lindsey find happiness – even if it was not with me – though I long for His mercy for our union. In all of these descriptions, when I say "piece of me" or "take my life," I mean "my essence." If we each have a finite amount of essence to give to everyone we can to help them find their way home, I wanted to express that I understood the concept and wanted to start subtracting quantifiable portions from my being in order to help others find happiness. All of this occurred on the first day of Spring on a blue sky, cloudless day.

28:7

"The Lord will grant that the enemies who rise up against you will be defeated before you. They will come at you from one direction but flee from you in seven."

— *Deuteronomy 28:7*

...

While the journal entry from the first day of Spring alluded to many different parts of the walk, the small reference to Deuteronomy 28:7 held a tremendous amount of significance. During this particular time of my journaling, I was mostly making sure to capture the highlights of each day, so I could go back (if need be) to further elaborate. For those who will continue to read the journals (Books IV – VII) after the first three books find their end, it is important to understand that, eventually, the journal entries do stand on their own – requiring little elaboration to tell the significance in the symbolism each one holds. But part of the journey was learning to see – and, in that, learning how to capture every little moment of the journey with utmost clarity.

On the first day of Spring, I received three written and signed job offers – each one filled with a potential new path to follow His lead. After having received the first two offers earlier in the day, I met with the third company's CEO, Wilson, at

Crowns

a coffee shop across the street from my home – a divinely symbolic moment to the journey with Lindsey. Wilson's company is a family-based business where I had already met with many of the employees at his family's office. During that first meeting, he opened a round-table discussion with a prayer. It was the first time I had ever witnessed the Spirit present in a business. It was a moment that will live on within me forever – a moment that I hope will live on forever through me to the readers. We had never spoken about the spiritual aspects of our journeys, though it seemed there was an unwritten understanding without words ever spoken. But it was during this first meeting that every word of the Spirit was said through the movement of the Lord's voice in the way the meeting was led.

When the day arrived that Wilson and I were to meet at the coffee shop to discuss the terms of the offer, our handshake was met with a similar divine gesture. The opening introduction in how Wilson chose to begin the meeting was by discussing a Bible verse that he had received in a text that morning. The verse was Deuteronomy 28:7. As it was written above, it can be seen that the verse is intended to serve as a battle cry for the Lord, a call to faith, an ode to a perfect forevermore. This particular verse ended with the reference to the number seven – a symbol I was just beginning to spiritually see with more frequency. It was as if the verse represented a circle's end. It began with the notation of verse 7 and ended with the word "seven."

As had been becoming evident in the way my Father's communication was occurring, the layers of meanings were becoming more visible for my spiritual eyes to see. Apart from the obvious spiritual implications of this job holding the blessing of my Father, there was so much more symbolism to uncover. Part of my prayers on the first day of Spring asked for peace and clarity in the dates of the trip for Lindsey and me. I had a tremendous amount of anxiety building up about whether there was enough time for her to complete reading the book before the trip. The dates chosen were the dates I believed were His intention, but there was still unrest in the unknowing. However, to be read verse 28:7 from Deuteronomy was my Father putting His arm around me. It was a time I heard Him say, "The 28th is correct. Just relax. You are doing great."

Gravity Calling was the first book of the journey – starting with how the darkness of my life compared to Genesis. The time I asked for help and was led on a journey in blindness was my version of Exodus. When I began to hear His voice calling, Leviticus became the portion of the journey I was on, which led me into the desert of Numbers, heading to the Promised Land. As Gravity Calling found its end, I was left standing with me feet in the sand – a metaphorical example to the ending of Numbers as Moses waited for the inheritance of God's promise. Deuteronomy is the fifth book of the Bible and the promise of Ever-After. It is the place where the journey reaches its end as the Israelites were led into the Promised Land. If there could ever have been a more divinely placed verse, I cannot imagine what it would have told. For in the moment I was shared Deuteronomy 28:7, it was as if God said everything about Lindsey, everything about the job, everything about the trip upcoming, and everything about the inheritance of the Promised Land foretold. And through all that was said, it was done so in the form of a battle cry of the Lord, sealed with His signature of the number seven where the beginning and the end of the circle were joined.

Through all of the majestic wonder that one verse held in a specific moment for me, it held additional meaning to Wilson as well. That is how the Spirit of the Lord works. For those who have ears to hear and eyes to see, the woven threads forming the fabric of existence are realized as hand-crafted with Love and carefully threaded by His hand. There are no mistakes. There is nothing imperfect or left unsaid. It is as it is intended to be, for each person to follow his individual journey's path as he learns how to run toward destiny. The verse that was given to me that day led me to accept the offer from Wilson and was the catalyst that enabled me to eventually move to Florida. And while that portion of the journey has now been revealed, there were still wondrous moments upcoming, leading up to Love's grand reveal.

After leaving the meeting with Wilson, I returned home to read chapter 28 from Deuteronomy. With every verse that has ever been shared with me, I have come to understand that the context from where a verse originated is equally as important. And while I will not elaborate on any further meanings of this chapter, I cannot help but smile at the way His hand helped this all transpire. The following section below includes the first

28:7

fourteen verses – seven on either side of the verse given – to chapter twenty-eight of Deuteronomy.

...

1 If you fully obey the Lord your God and carefully follow all his commands I give you today, the Lord your God will set you high above all the nations on Earth. 2 All these blessings will come on you and accompany you if you obey the Lord your God:

3 You will be blessed in the city and blessed in the country.

4 The fruit of your womb will be blessed, and the crops of your land and the young of your livestock—the calves of your herds and the lambs of your flocks.

5 Your basket and your kneading trough will be blessed.

6 You will be blessed when you come in and blessed when you go out.

7 The Lord will grant that the enemies who rise up against you will be defeated before you. They will come at you from one direction but flee from you in seven.

8 The Lord will send a blessing on your barns and on everything you put your hand to. The Lord your God will bless you in the land he is giving you.

9 The Lord will establish you as his holy people, as he promised you on oath, if you keep the commands of the Lord your God and walk in obedience to him. 10 Then all the peoples on Earth will see that you are called by the name of the Lord, and they will fear you. 11 The Lord will grant you abundant prosperity—in the fruit of your womb, the young of your livestock and the crops of your ground—in the land he swore to your ancestors to give you.

Crowns

12 The Lord will open the heavens, the storehouse of his bounty, to send rain on your land in season and to bless all the work of your hands. You will lend to many nations but will borrow from none. 13 The Lord will make you the head, not the tail. If you pay attention to the commands of the Lord your God that I give you this day and carefully follow them, you will always be at the top, never at the bottom. 14 Do not turn aside from any of the commands I give you today, to the right or to the left, following other gods and serving them.

- Deuteronomy 28:1-14

When In Rome

"For Rome!" as it was shouted out.

"For Rome," they replied.

The peace instilled within me on the first day of Spring through the verses of Deuteronomy 28 was the result of a spiritual battle cry for the Promised Land that awaited. It was the voice of my Father shouting from the distance. It was the voice of Love in gentle disposition. It was the resounding resonance of a war hymn played upon the battlefield before two sides clash. It was a kiss on the lips from a Loved one before deployment. It was the words, "Be safe. No goodbyes. You will make it back. I will see you soon." It was notes packed in a knapsack to be discovered and reminded of Home. It was the simple look in the eyes where no words were spoken. It was a finger on the lips shooshing the other. It was the sound of the taxi arriving at the door. It was a last embrace of innocence before changes from war.

Just like the ideals of the glory of Rome, so too were the ideals of the Promised Land of the Lord. From the earliest days the Roman city existed, it represented the idea of striving for perfection. It was not a city that was stagnant; it was a city in motion. The name of the city did not represent a location, for it was the idea of the perfection that was brought to mind when spoken. It is the only city in documented history that chased after an ideal and attempted to instill that concept within its people. But unfortunately, it eventually became corrupt and unraveled giving victory to the darkness in the spiritual battle.

Perhaps the idea of Rome was garnered, in part, from the archetype of the Lord's perfection: a city of Love, a city of divine essence. But just as the changes in languages were occurring and the attempts at corralling society through politics and deceit in religion began nurturing the ego, the concepts of archetypes fell by the wayside. When the very foundational pieces to the divine architecture of All were lost, it created chaos in the midst of every action. Man became slave to the ego and slave to dominion, while the spirit was repressed and, though actively practiced, essentially decommissioned. Without foundation, structure becomes unstable as it falls to the mercy of ego. So too did the ancient city of Rome fall, and with it the archetypal ideals of the spiritual call.

There are references throughout the Bible that speak of great cities that became corrupt throughout the ages. When they are referenced in the Bible, they are often taken quite literally instead of being seen for the archetypal meaning. One of these cities was Sodom. Another country mentioned in archetypal form was Egypt. Both of these locations represented mankind's attempts at perfection. But often when pastors, historians, and theologians study written history, the analysis is created without the foundation with which it was written.

When In Rome

Egypt represented a form of wealth and power. Sodom represented a great city like Rome during the ages. Both became corrupt and became victims of great destruction, handed down by the judgment of God upon their nations. But if the cities can be seen as archetypal concepts, it could easily be understood how the concepts transcend into a person. For if the body is the temple for the Spirit – a house for the soul that is part of a city – the ideals of "Rome," "Sodom," and "Egypt" represent the striving for perfection corrupted by ego and selfish reason. Though Sodom is often thought about for the homosexual discretion, the concept of homosexuality is archetypal for Love of self and Love of the ego. These words are not intended to create divide in such a polarizing topic of a person's orientation, but rather to help bring rationale to a long forgotten foundation. To understand the references of once great cities are used in a way to illustrate much grander concepts is one of the ways required to understand Divine language.

In the Book of Revelation, John speaks of two witnesses who will prepare the way for the return of the Messiah. Most of these verses are taken quite literally, though Revelation is meant to be understood archetypally. He says in verses 11:7-8:

...

"Now when they have finished their testimony, the beast that comes up from the Abyss will attack them, and overpower and kill them. Their bodies will lie in the public square of the great city – which is figuratively called Sodom and Egypt – where also their Lord was crucified."

...

Crowns

The last verse he mentions figurative locations called Sodom and Egypt. Until it is understood that Sodom and Egypt are archetypal for the battle of the soul and the ego, in a location that is also a symbolic battlefield, many will miss the greater story intended to be shared. Where was the Lord crucified? In the flesh of the body before the people who had built great cities, economies, and all of the things that promote the Love of self versus the Love of others through the Love of Christ...the city of Sodom – a homosexual earthly paradise. For those uncomfortable with the reference to homosexuality, similar ideas can be explored through "the fall of Babylon" as the "whore of humanity." The same type of symbolism can be seen in the Biblical references to pregnant women and the multitude of references to women as whores in general. And while the spiritual form will always manifest in physical representation, it is always the spiritual archetype at the very foundation.

Deuteronomy 28 was the promise of Forever in a land that He had prepared for those that followed His call. The description of the land is literally manifest as the homeland of the Israelites though the figurative representation is in the Love of Christ. The entire chapter discusses the rules of following Him versus disobeying His command. It explains all that He will provide, and what will cause it to be taken away. The Love I saw in Lindsey – the Love Story being told – was a symbolic journey across the Torah, a perfect romance to one day experience when in Rome. My Father had prepared an immaculate conception for the rebirth of my soul as I sought to follow His directions that were leading me Home.

Heading into the weekend of the 22nd – a day symbolic to "divinity," "choice," and "completion" in the archetypal progression – I hoped Lindsey would finish reading Gravity Calling. As I prayed for continued peace and acceptance of the outcome, my Father continued to speak to me through His angels and travels to the heavens. On the morning of March 22nd, I would once again be taken to the heavens where my soul would experience an archetypal presentation of the battle of the ego and the soul occurring within Lindsey over a flooded city of Rome. My journal entry is as follows:

...

March 22, 2014

I found myself standing in a location called "Rome." I do not know if I was in Rome, Italy or Rome, Georgia – but my first impression was Rome, Georgia. However, in retrospect, I think "Rome" was actually intended to be the archetype for "advanced civilization." The city was slowly being flooded. There was one angelic couple who was looking for houses to purchase. I journeyed around with them in areas where the water had not reached. There were street names given to me along the way. They were important because they represented more symbolically than the street name itself. One street began with the letter N, though I do not remember the word. The other street was "Falling Down Street."

During the time spent with the angelic couple, Lindsey was with me. Eventually, Lindsey and I were put in a simple rowboat that could hold somewhere between four and six people. I rowed her through the water. I knew the water we were in was covering a partially submerged "New Rome" though it was not as deep as the water ahead of me. As we continued to row, I left "New Rome" and rowed into the part of the water that covered "Old Rome" – which was much deeper and more ominous.

While we were over one of the deepest parts, Lindsey wanted to get out and walk to the shore. For some reason, she thought we were in shallow water. She did not understand the heavens, nor the water we were in. The body of water we were in was very dangerous and I knew that no one should attempt to even swim in it. When she stepped to the edge of the boat, I began shouting at her not to step off the boat. She plunged into the depths at a rate quicker than I can begin to describe. I immediately jumped in, knowing I was placing myself at risk. I could swim faster than she was falling. It was as if she was being sucked into the depths of eternal nothingness.

As I swam, I saw the submerged city/world that the water was covering. I swam approximately fifty feet before I managed to get underneath her and tried to hold her up. As I pushed upward, I could not do anything more than balance her in the water. I was quickly running out of oxygen due to the depth and the amount of effort I was taking.

Suddenly, an angel dove in and swam down to help. He was joined by another male angel. They told me to go to the surface to get air. I swam up while they tried to pull her up. When I reached the surface, I was floundering, but was managing to stay afloat. The pull under the water was strong, but I was stronger and could fight it to stay afloat. There was one more angel on the shore that said we would take turns diving in and helping out.

In a very short conversation, I asked what was happening to her. He said that she sank because of "something that happened before the flood."

When In Rome

He jumped in to help the other two angels. I reached the shore to pull myself out. We rotated jumping in to help pull her up. In the fury of the moment, I lost harmony, and returned to my body. I immediately prayed to God asking Him to help save her, and that I wanted to get back to save her.

Rituals

On the evening of March 22nd, still unsure of the meaning of the experience in the heavens with the sunken city of Rome and Lindsey from earlier in the morning, I attended an old friend's wedding reception. It was a celebration I was not sure I wanted to attend for even though the chance was slight, I wanted to avoid any chance of seeing Lindsey that night. I knew she used to run around in our circle of friends, and though we never saw each other except for that one initial occasion, I knew with so much time passing and the amount of people invited to the reception, there was a good chance our paths could cross. In any other circumstance, it would be a welcomed happenchance. But with having given Lindsey the book to read, I wanted the best chance for the rest of the story to play out to the Grand Ballroom in the fairytale ending. But perhaps the irony was in the ballroom itself, for as it would turn out, the wedding reception was held in the Grand Ballroom of a private club in town. Though my intention was to be in and out after exchanging pleasantries, the brevity was a little longer than I expected.

  The night was filled with catching up with old friends. Many I had not seen in quite a while since I had removed myself from social functions after embarking upon the journey. It was an interesting perspective in returning after two years of absence. However, it was good to catch up nonetheless. I refrained from drinking since I wanted to commune in the heavens with the angels later that evening. Perhaps that caused a form of divide or maybe it was just my absence for the last two years – but regardless, maintaining conversations seemed to be a struggle – something I was unaccustomed to.

I was able to find conversation with an old friend who drove in from out-of-town. I could tell she was also struggling with similar circumstances and was feeling left out. We talked about the bride and the groom and how happy we were for them. We talked for quite a while and caught up on the past few years. The topic of relationships came up; she was at peace; she was happy. She asked about me. I responded in kind, but without names and in brevity. The rituals we had once experienced with friends now seemed so empty. We both recognized it, but the words were never said.

And perhaps "ritual" is an appropriate term because it was apparent in the Grand Ballroom in the presence of friends that once were, that the Waltz of Ever-After would never have occurred without seeking my Father and leaving behind the earthly world. The "things that people do" when they get together in the company of friends is almost certainly a demonstration of ego rather than a dance with the spirit…and, in that, the very definition of a ritual is formed. To me, I see a ritual as the embodiment of repeated efforts in hard construct and absence of the Spirit. Since the Spirit is ever-flowing and

Rituals

like water in form, to have a ritual defies the motion of the Lord.

As I pondered this thought on rituals and the conversation continued with my friend, everything in the room suddenly came to a standstill. Perhaps everyone else continued on in motion, but for me, the world completely stopped moving. It was like a scene in a movie where a person walks through a frozen montage of people, mesmerized at the absence of motion. With the world at a standstill, I watched as Lindsey entered the building. She was wearing a black dress and looked indescribably perfect.

It was the Grand Ballroom and we were together, in a social scene reminiscent of the ending to the Love Story being written. While it was evident she was there to meet a number of her friends, I tried not to let her see me notice her – as hard as it was. The scene of the Ballroom, the dress she wearing, the company of friends that greeted her when she entered – this was a scene my Father had shown me in the weeks prior during the foreshadowing of His unveiling. Though it may seem difficult to believe, I was reliving a moment I had already seen. The time eventually arrived when we made eye contact, just as I had been shown. She smiled and waved hello. She finished her conversation with her friends and moved in the direction I was standing.

I smiled and said it was "good to see you again." I asked her how she was doing and if she had finished the reading. It was not the exact circumstance I had desired to occur, but I made the best of it and tried to keep our conversation short.

Crowns

Lindsey said she had just finished the book, and went on to tell me how her friends knew about the story too. She told me how they were excited and anxious to see what was ahead, though she had not had a chance to make it to the bank yet. With that comment and knowing the trip was less than a week away, I let her know that the contents were time-sensitive, but not to hurry. I'm sure that captured her curiosity because she continued to ask me what I meant, but I wanted to leave a mystery behind to her question before I left.

Our conversation was short – maybe only sixty seconds at most – before I said goodbye and headed on Home. The walk from the building back to my Jeep was perhaps the longest walk I had ever experienced. Though I had only parked a couple blocks away, my heart was racing with questions. Maybe it was just my nerves and anxiety that was getting the best of me, but the evening was a bit unexpected as was the symbolism of seeing Lindsey in a Grand Ballroom at a wedding reception while wearing a black dress.

Over the previous weeks my mind had been filled with every possibility with Lindsey. Sometimes I would experience grand moments like dancing with her soul in the heavens as the angels encircled us and watched on Lovingly. There were other times that I would have flashes of everything falling to pieces. Though my journals do not capture all of the back-and-forth emotions, it stretched my emotional capacity to its limits. Truthfully, I thought I was losing my mind. It seemed only rational to assume I had. But after the night of the wedding reception, seeing her in a black dress, and the symbolism

Rituals

I witnessed, I knew my Father was both preparing me and testing me in my acceptance of all of the endings that could be penned by His hand – from the small to the grand. Though my heart was breaking out in a riot, the only thing I could do was find stature in His promise. So with my feet planted firmly in the sand, I straightened my posture, stood tall, and gazed upon the Promised Land.

As A King

Throughout the Love story being written, I continually prayed for my Father to groom me as a king. The prayers were not driven for selfish or earthly reasons. Rather, it should be seen that when there is an ideal to strive toward, it is the call of every individual to strive for it. For to be a king not of the earthly world, is to see through the eyes of the Spirit and understand a spiritual Love greater than the Love on Earth. And make no mistake, to be a king one must still be crowned. It is not just an idea, but a spiritual ideal to be sought and found. It is through these humbled prayers and continued perseverance that on March 24th, I was blessed with an amazing experience. At the time I would not see how it corresponded to the journey with Lindsey. But perhaps the story with Lindsey at the time had me blinder-locked to earthly Love as I chased Ever-After, for the real story was His Story and a spiritual child being born into the heavens.

On March 24th, in the wake of having seen Lindsey in the Grand Ballroom of the wedding reception, I held on to hope that, in the coming days, she would have the courage to open the safety deposit box. I had worked it out with the bank that I would be informed when she arrived, in order to know if I could head to Florida a few days early or if I should try to reschedule her family's flights. When Monday arrived and the bank opened for business, the minutes that passed seemed like an eternity of time for my soul to experience. At lunchtime I drove to the soccer field between the three churches where I find solitude to pray and spent the next hour in deep prayer and meditation. It was during this time my Father spoke to me in His grandest way. It was the type of the experience which would take some time for me to understand in its entirety, but even so, it was the moment I began to understand His greater intentions for me. Though "The Greatest Love Story Ever Told" was still being written, this was the time I began to see His Love Story's transcendence. This is the account as written in my journal after it occurred:

...

March 24, 2014

Today may be the most significant day I have ever experienced during my journey. While I had several experiences in the heavens, I was unable to bring them back with me. But, as I began my day, there was an air of peace and calm. It felt as if everything around me was in perfect balance. Last night, Bryan and I had a conversation where he felt very inclined to tell me about a new way of worship he was practicing. He was beginning each day in silence to allow God the opportunity to speak to him, rather than just pray and ask for a response. While I am sure on the outside, this may appear to be where "voices in the head" would be the popularly categorized explanation of this, please understand that there is a distinction between hearing voices and understanding how to listen for the voice of God.

As A King

  Bryan explained to me several of the things imparted to him over the last several days. He was concerned I would think he was losing his mind, but I fully understood and accepted the idea that a conversation can be had with God internally versus externally. After all, prayers can be said in the mind. We also discussed how this offsets the potential for communication with God becoming ritual versus fluid, because this allows an open opportunity for communication in addition to the communication that is had throughout the day.

  So, after reflecting on our conversation, I decided that I would attempt the same thing today. During lunch, I drove to my special place among the soccer fields near the three churches in Brentwood, Tennessee. I ate my lunch in silence. Afterwards, I prayed aloud to God explaining what I was going to try to attempt to do through silence. I reclined my seat in my Jeep and closed my eyes. As soon as I shut my eyes I thought the following sentence in my mind, "So, God. I assume this is how this is supposed to happen. I am just supposed to think about how I want to communicate with You and You will speak. So this is me listening for Your voice."

  As instantly as I had completed the last word of that sentence in my thoughts, my phone rang. My first thought was that this must be the bank letting me know Lindsey finally arrived for the items I left for her in the safety deposit box. I smiled as I reached for my phone. Sure enough, it was an 855 number that could be the bank calling. I answered and only heard the tail end of a recorded message. The only thing that was heard when I clicked answer on my phone was, "664. Thank you."

  It was obviously the tail end of a recorded message, but here is where it gets good. 664 reduces to seven (6+6+4 = 16, which 1 + 6 = 7) – the continued way that God communicates with me. As I say this, it does

Crowns

not mean that God communicates that way with everyone, or maybe even anyone else — but I know this is the way I have learned to listen for His voice. So as I sat there in disbelief, I processed the conversation that had just occurred. I said, "So this is me listening for Your voice." And God replied with a means he knew I would understand — the number seven.

Perhaps it held a dual meaning letting me know that at 12:08 p.m. Lindsey might have checked the safety deposit box as well — but, the overriding message was God's reply to my voice inside. This was the moment that marked seeing the inside in the same way as I see the outside — the final dimensional understanding of seeing the spiritual and earthly worlds as one. In spiritual texts, it is always said that one must learn to see both the heavens and the Earth as one and the inside the same as the outside. Today was the day of seeing the outside internally.

The day had already begun with this type of communication occurring to me multiple times, but this was the first time that it occurred in conversation with Him. Usually it is understanding when to take action by listening for His voice. But this time was different. As I sat there, I was overcome with emotion, but I pressed onward.

I shut my eyes and began to have fluent conversation in my mind with Him. As I spoke, I began to receive answers — but answers unlike anything I would have expected. I began to see internalized images imparted to me through this "wormhole" (as Bryan described it). I found myself being told to drive some form of spherical vehicle. It was a sphere that was part of three spheres spinning around themselves. I was told to just drive and not to open my eyes — just to listen for His voice.

In this moment, I did as I was asked and as I drove the vehicle down the road, I saw two birds and a carwash and came to a stop. In my mind, I heard, "Two birds on the carwash. Good." My mind was split in an

As A King

earthly/spiritual duality. I could process what was going on in my mind, but was having a spiritual conversation inside. This is by far the hardest thing I have ever tried to explain in writing — but at this point I can only imagine a nonbeliever would think I am mad, and a believer would hold hope that what I am writing is correct. For me, this is truth and the unmistakably divine architecture to life.

As I sat there thinking about the two birds and the carwash, I recognized I understood the two birds, but had no idea what the purpose of the carwash was in the vision. As I thought about it, I heard a voice, "Follow me." Immediately, I began to journey down this "wormhole" and images started to fill my mind. I was only allowed to see certain parts of the location. The rest was intentionally shielded from view.

We walked into a room. I could not tell you who was leading me, only that I was being led. I was walked into a section of seats of which the seat on my left hand side (which would be the right hand side of the section) was brought directly into my view. It was clearly the "right hand side" chair because the design of the chair demonstrated an arching armrest on its right hand side and a flat side to its left, which was adjoining to something else, though it was shielded from view.

As I began to observe the intricacies of the chair, I heard, "This is your [insert word for seat/chair/place of rest]." I do not know exactly what the last word was because it held a connotation I had not heard before. All I knew was that I was told that it was my [seat]. As I observed the chair, I noticed that it was made of a plush grayish-lavender fabric. In the middle of the back of the seat were three letters all in uppercase script. The letters were T-A-J.

I thought about the letters. My mind raced back to being imparted the word "Teja" a year or so ago (that is my spelling — all I truly know is that it was pronounced TAY-YAH). I wondered if I did not understand how the word was spelled. Then I began to wonder if it was my spiritual name — though I had recently been called by my earthly name in the heavens. As I continued to observe this split spiritual/earthly duality of my mind, I began to think about the archetypes of the letters. I immediately recognized the importance of the letters. The first letter represented divinity. The second letter represented the strength of God. The last letter indicated right hand of God. These are the three most important archetypes that underlie the base of Hebrew, and I began to realize that I must be being shared a word that I did not know yet.

Eventually I pulled myself back into my earthly mind, though I felt like I was in a blissful world for quite a while after opening my eyes. I decided to google the word. Instantly, I realized that it was the beginning to the word Taj Mahal — the religious building in India. Still, I had no idea what it meant. I looked up the word and discovered that the origin of the word was Sanskrit. This should come as no surprise to me anymore. I continually am imparted Sanskrit words though I have never read anything about the language itself. I have only come to understand that its basis is the same as the Hebrew archetypes. So, as I read the meaning of the word, I was overcome with such a moment that the heavens stood still around me. The word means "crown."

As my journey has progressed, I have continually asked God to groom me as a king (whether I am ever to reach that level or not). Receiving a crown in the Bible is not the same as popular culture would lead a person to believe. It is more of a recognition of God's recognition in your walk and that He is in you. Essentially, today I found the Kingdom within and was told by God that I was a King. There are no words that can do this justice. There is nothing I can write that can express the gravity of this moment. Honestly, I have no ability to demonstrate anything other than the conversation I had in words, for I have been shown that I am a King of a Kingdom not of this Earth. And with that, I have to assume the word that was imparted to me for the seat meant "throne" or some variation thereof. I can only surmise that when I was shown how the seat joined to something to its left, it would indicate something similar to the name of YHWH, which means "the right hand of revelation of the nail of revelation." I have a hard time even putting this into words because of how the implications could be misconstrued – or possibly there is nothing to misconstrue. This is what happened to me, and it is the grandest moment of my spiritual journey.

Day of Reckoning

There is a moment when a person's faith is tested beyond its bounds. There is a time when all seems lost until a precise moment of Divine intervention occurs and leaves the soul utterly spellbound. I think the only way I can describe this test placed upon the journey is to compare it to the story of Abraham and Isaac. There is a time in the Torah that God calls Abraham – the father of every religion to this generation of mankind – to take an unbelievable leap of faith in demonstration of His Love for God.

In that call from God, Abraham is asked to build an altar and make a sacrifice upon a mountaintop. That sacrifice would be to take his only son born unto his wife Sarah and sacrifice his life in demonstration of his Love and obedience. Though Abraham did not want to follow God's will, he knew he had no choice. As he tied Isaac down upon the altar and raised the blade above His head, the Lord called out from the heavens and said, "Abraham. Do not lay a hand on the boy. Do not do anything to him. Now I know that you fear God, because you have not withheld from me your son, your only son." With those words, the Lord sent a ram to be sacrificed in Isaac's place.

Crowns

While my experience is nowhere near a moment of life and death, it is the only comparison that can be made when the sacrifice that you have been tasked to make before God involves the most vulnerable part of your being. For Abraham, it was the Love of his son. For the time period it occurred, the demonstration of the sacrifice of a soul's Love had to be expressed in the most animalistic means. For before Abraham, there was no other whom God had shown more favor during mankind's time.

The record of Abraham and Isaac is written about in the twenty-second chapter of Genesis. And as it was revealed earlier in this book, and as it will eventually be revealed through the study of the Books of Nine as One, the twenty-second archetype – the twenty-second letter of the Hebrew alphabet – represents a decision, a choice in God. The choice that is made is a test of faith and a demonstration of the completion of the first part of the journey. For after this test, faith can be seen as Divine in His eyes.

The twenty-second letter of the Hebrew alphabet is Tav. It was originally portrayed in picture form as a cross. And while it represents a choice, it is the point where the beginning and end of a circle meet, or meet their ends. In modern times, mankind understands the Greek phrase "the Alpha and the Omega" as a name for God meaning "the Beginning and the End." The original Hebrew version of this verse is actually "the Aleph and the Tav," the first and last letters of the alphabet, the All and the Divine, the circle that is complete. But

Day of Reckoning

above all, the twenty-second letter is the choice one makes as to how the next part of His story shall be told.

For me, the place I was most vulnerable was the Love held within my soul. In Gravity Calling, I explain how my soul had once been broken and shattered into a million pieces from my marriage that had ended before. It had taken me years to rebuild the framework of the man I once was, and ultimately would never again be. I was fragile, broken, and humbled before Him. The Love from within was my greatest point of vulnerability, for I knew that if I followed all that He willed and the lesson ended without the ending I desired, then my soul would undoubtedly shatter across the floor into an unrecognizable essence of someone that once was, and would never be forever more.

If there was one thing I could not give, it was the Love from pounding within my soul. But that is the test He used on me to gauge the strength of my Love for Him. Whether I was willing to follow every lead that he gave and place my soul in the ultimate place of vulnerability, that is everything – the complete package of my being – that I could possibly give to Him. In modern times, His test could only be done in this kind of way, for modern man must see a demonstration of faith in a way he can understand. If the same test of Abraham was to be rehashed in this generation, it would have to be in a way that no one would have expected to come. So when my personal Day of Reckoning arrived in the Love story being written, let it be known that this was the leap of faith where I jumped, and He caught me in His hands.

Perspective

Sometimes the greatest way to tell the experience of a story is to do so from the perspective as it happened. Books IV – VII capture the journaled accounts of the entire journey and can be read in this fashion. But in Books I – III, the story is told through the perspective of a Love story with Lindsey. When I was initially led into the desert with the Promised Land in sight, I thought the story was about her and the destination of Love my Father had in store for my life. Every part of the journey leading up to my Day of Reckoning, was preparing me for my Abraham and Isaac moment – a testament of my faith. So instead of recounting the events of the way the Love story played out, perhaps it is best for the reader to experience it, as I experienced it, with all of the emotions as I wrote it down. Below is the unedited entry from my journal on my Day of Reckoning.

...

March 24, 2014
Late Evening

Yesterday I received a text from Lindsey thanking me for the gesture, but letting me know that she did not feel comfortable going to the bank or accepting the contents of the safety deposit box. As soon as I received that text, my heart sank. I cannot say I did not expect it at all — I still had high hopes that God would provide an improbable solution to the seemingly unraveling future with her. I held strong. Over the past few weeks I knew the day would come where I would see her with Chris.

It hurt. No doubt it hurt. But, as I sat there soaking it all in, I mustered up the only reply I could and told her I understood and asked her to return the key and book to a post office box I have for my company. Her text left me feeling like she was uncomfortable with everything I had written. That was not exactly the response I was looking for, but I have to believe an idea was planted. Yesterday, Lindsey had posted on twitter a quote saying something along the lines of "Sometimes we want God to provide for us, but only on our own time." It was interesting to see because it acknowledged that she understood Him reaching His hand out to her, but that she was resistant to the idea.

So after I replied back to her text, I sat on my couch in the darkness thinking about everything. I wrestled with the idea that either I was losing my mind, or that there was a purpose in what had happened. If anything, I felt more peace than any other feeling. I sat there numb to the surroundings just trying to digest it all. There were moments I felt sick to my stomach, and moments where I breathed a sigh of relief. All in all, I did not expect to feel the way I felt because the slew of emotions tossed around inside of me over the previous months had left me feeling rather helpless and broken at times. I could only expect this time I would be broken again. But I was not. Instead I was confused and introspective.

As I thought about how the book ended with her holding a key housed in clay and the remains of a bookmark that revealed a soul within, I searched for reason. Clearly God has been speaking to me this whole time. Clearly He has continued to show me undeniably amazing experiences in the heavens and with angels here on Earth. I actually started praying aloud for God to just turn off this messed up world and bring me up to heaven.

Let me underscore that it was not me asking for death, but rather for life. I wanted Him to just reveal everything because I no longer understood any part of it. My only options remaining in order to continue on during my earthly journey were: (1) to dismiss it all, suppress all that I thought I had been shown, and go back to just living life like all of the other oblivious people or (2) to accept the outcome as His will and continue onward on His path.

That was it. Those were the only two options. Nothing in between. This was a line drawn in the sand where I had to choose. Earlier in the day, God showed me I was a King. But I sat on my couch struggling with one single overarching concept that caused me to question everything: that concept was that I had no tangible proof of anything, which means it is all in my head.

I am probably one of the most analytical and reasonable people when it comes to unclouded and unbiased thought. So, as I sat on my couch in the darkness trying to rationalize everything, I honestly found myself lost again. I could understand that the money spent on all of the arrangements for Lindsey's future was purposed into my life by God — so I could not be mad about spending it that way. I could understand all of the work He and the angels had shown me manifested in ways that would mount a defense that would withstand the toughest prosecutor. I would revisit the option of turning away from God, where it would seem that the only outcome was for a person to waste away on Earth.

Eventually I began to see that Lindsey — more importantly identified as the spiritual recognition of its counterpoint in another — was revealed a *key to Ever-After, a life that would never have wants nor needs in any aspect. The overflowing demonstration of God providing an unquantifiable number of financial, emotional, and spiritual gifts for her future was apparent. Most importantly, the key was housed in clay. I began to see that this ever so important ending to the book that I was led to write, was intended for me to see and witness its significance. For if I were to continue on to the Promised Land, I would need to better understand the definition as the Kingdom of Eternal Love.*

To paraphrase the ending of the book, a soul was revealed the potential for a Love greater than it had ever known. The soul was shown that there was a key housed within the clay – symbolic to the body of the human – where all the person had to do was open the box. Instead, this soul chose to not open the box – to not even look inside. The only potential was greatness, and instead they feared what they saw. They feared the abundance being provided for them. In essence, the box contained a future of no wants and no worries for the rest of all time.

If I was to parallel this portion of my journey as a trial of being groomed as a King, this must be how God feels when He says to each person – "Here, I will offer you the Kingdom and everything within it. I will offer you perfection, Ever-After and a lifetime of beauty and Love. It is everything you thought you wanted and desired, plus much more. In fact, I will show you how to find it – how to find Me. There is a key within your body. All you have to do is use it. I will show you where the key is. I will tell you who I Am. I will even tell you what it unlocks and where to find it. The only action you have to take is to open the box."

It was then that I got it. I understood. Not only was it a parallel to all that God has offered through His words, through His message delivered through others in finding Him. But, it was a parallel to my earlier moment

Perspective

of Him showing me my seat as a King. On 3/24/2014, I was shown the Kingdom. This was the same day that Lindsey was shown the Kingdom on Earth — every spiritual truth manifested in a way for a perfect life during her earthly walk. All she had to do was open the box. All I had to do was observe the dualities and choose to follow or return to before I was once saved. It was then as I thought about the dualities, that I also recognized again that Heaven and Earth are one. For, a person must see above as below, and the outer as the inner. I was witnessing everything in that moment as a testament to my walk. And as I thought about all that Lindsey was walking away from — all I could think about was how dumb it was not to open the box to see what was within.

With a blind arrogance and not even a desire to see, she chose the mundane over the ineffable. And in that, I knew I had no choice. My choice had been made long ago. I was not angry at her. In fact, I was heartbroken for her — not for me. It was the first time I have ever experienced this feeling, and it must be what spiritual Love feels like when it is lost. Because all I could feel was sadness for her — sadness that she did not even open the box. And while I thought about everything further, I realized that the ending I had written to the book that was intentionally left out of the ending to Lindsey's version of the book — the real ending which was sealed in an envelope that resided in the box she was to open — was only a potential of all that could be if she just sought to chase Love — and through that find God's ever-warming Love in His arms wrapped around her.

This was also the moment when I recognized how God must feel when someone turns away from Him. A person who has not been shown the key has somewhat of a larger playground to stumble and fall. Perhaps, God does not even judge them at all until they begin to see glimmers. And only then, when they have been shown the key, is a soul judged. This is all

Crowns

that is told in Deuteronomy 28. This is the verse I was given the day I signed my contract with Wilson. In this very moment, I was not witnessing my life fall apart — I was witnessing it fall together. This was the time that God said, "Here is the key. I've shown you the key. I've shown you everything I can to get you there. Now it is up to you to choose to use the key." And in that moment, I chose God. The day that God showed me the key and the day I chose to use it occurred on a day of His divine signs for me — 3/24/2014 — which adds to $3+2+4+2+0+1+4 = 16$, which totals $1+6 = 7$. Today was divine.

A Place For Everything

It was revealed to me early upon the journey that writing was an important aspect of becoming. In order to truly discover the Love of my Father as He always intended me to discover, I had to make sure I captured everything in the way precisely as it was said so I could one day look back and see all that I had missed and all that was always there. It is an interesting thing to see in hindsight how the body was used as a vessel in times ego seemed to be hanging on. But I came to realize as the journey unfolded that He works through each and everyone – at all times, regardless of the outcomes. Sometimes the outcome is everything that was expected. To those, they can receive peace and comfort. But for those that push for more, the outcome will never be as expected. It will always be so much more. In that, I came to understand that the journey in the Love story with Lindsey was a greater story my Father was telling all along. It was His Story, His Proclamation, His gravity calling me Home.

When Gravity Calling was written, I thought there would only be one book in the series. I never expected the journals, the songs, the poetry, and the future parts to still unfold to be anything more than a romance of the soul. And really, it was not. But it Was. The journey became nine books that would tell an even greater story than I thought was being told when I took my first step while learning to walk in the rebirth of my soul. The first book was a story painted from the palette of Love's romantic hues. The second book revealed the crowning of a soul being rebirthed into the world. The third book is truly Ever-After, and the fairytale ending He always planned for me to see – the Love Story's ending written for all of the world to find faith in and believe. Books IV – VII tell the story as captured through my journals through the eyes of a child learning to see. Book VIII is the story of the architecture of All – the heavens and the Earth – though it is the most difficult to read. Book IX is a book of songs, prose, inspirations, and maxims to serve as the melody of the words written. And while each book can be read individually, when understood as a whole, there is an even more remarkable story being told.

While it is important to understand that God's intentions will always be unveiled through layers of meaning over time, it should be understood that there is a reason and a place for everything in the way He leads a vessel to write. These books – as they were written – should be left untouched in words and form in order to maintain the truest white of His Light. Some aspects of the symbolism in the words were revealed to me in the beginning while other parts were revealed in the middle. But in the end, more will be revealed than even I was led to see. Though this is just the second book in the series of the Books of Nine, it was the last book written, with this chapter being the twenty-seventh and last one completed. But for the

A Place For Everything

depth of the words to begin to be understood, it is important to bring to the light the broadest parts of His divine symbolism.

It should be seen that the number of pages in each book, holds a specific significance to the meaning carried in the words. The page numbers, while different than the physical page numbers (due to the Roman numeral beginning), carry a numeric significance just as the actual page number it is printed upon. Every book leads with an introduction that is printed on page vii, which is both the physical and numeric page upon which they were printed. The total numbers of pages in each book, are also just as important. Gravity Calling contains 314 pages – a meaning symbolic to Pi and the divinity in the circle. Seven of the books, contain page counts that reduce-sum to seven. Those books are II, III, IV, V, VI, VIII, and IX. Book VII is 382 pages, which is equals 13, the number of Love, a book represented by the color red and is titled Glory.

The colors of the books are the colors revealed in Book VIII, that reveal the underlying architecture of the universe and the meanings of each. While a rainbow has seven colors, it is only a portion of the whole. Nine colors truly exist, two only visible to the soul. The two books that contain the colors representing these hidden hues, are the two most important books of the journey for these two books reveal all that is hidden upon the journey to Love and in finding Christ within. These two books are revealed by counting in reverse to the Divine scale of God, starting at Book VII, the third from the end – the beginning of the circle, leading to the circle's end. As it will be revealed through the Divine scale, Book III and Book VIII are

Crowns

the two books that contain the hidden part of the journey which were always intended to be revealed in a specific way – the full extent of that revelation is in Book III which drew to completion a journey of 1260 days.

Book I contains 46 chapters. Book II contains 27. These are the same number of Books in the Old Testament and New. It should also be seen that 27 is 3 x 9, the Trinity of Completion. Book III contains 44 chapters, a double of the number 22. The explanation of these numbers can be found in the respective verses housed in "The Hidden Words of Bahá'u'lláh," an ancient book of the Baha'i faith. It is a faith practiced mostly in the Middle East and Asia, a faith which represents spiritual unity throughout mankind. In the book previously mentioned, it can be found that 22 represents the Son of the Spirit (In Hebrew, it is the same meaning representing the completion of Divinity's arc), while 44 holds the meaning of The Son of the Throne also known and The Chosen One. Book III contains 448 pages, where the number 44 is demonstrated in the first two numbers. When added together, 4+4 = 8. And 8 + 8 = 16. It is an important number throughout spirituality. 1 and 6 represent the Spirit plus Man, which then sums to seven, the signature of God's divine hand.

The Books of Nine are divided into three trinities. Books I – III should be seen as a metaphorical journey through the trinity of the Old Testament, the New, and All That Is And Was To Come In Christ's Return. These three books also carry the meaning of the journey through the Divine Trinity: the Father, the Son, and the Holy Ghost. This can be visualized through the themes of being shown directive, learning to see, and baptism. Gravity Calling contains 49 total sections which is comprised of three hidden among 46 chapters. The three hidden within represent the Father, the Son, and the Holy Ghost. The middle three books are the journals entitled Rebirth. While Book VII is the final book of journals, it is divided by name for its placement in another section, for it should also be grouped in the Books of Divine Inspiration. Books IV – VII contain seven revelations. The first three books each contain one, while Book VII contains the final four.

There is a story divided through Books III – VII, in how the chapter entitled Wonders is divided into five parts. It begins in Book IV, but ends its fifth section by returning to the start of the ordered books. These five divisions are representative of the five books of the Torah which was the theme of the journey defined in Gravity Calling. The four books of journals, Books IV – VII, should be seen in a metaphorical context to the first four Gospels. Books VIII and IX should be seen akin to Acts and Revelation in that they both fall slightly out of the canonical groupings.

It should be seen that Book I took the longest to write and did not begin until my thirtieth year of life. Books II and III were the last books written completed just before the final day of my thirty-third year. Book III was written in the first twenty-eight days of March 2015, symbolic to the cycle of the moon and the first day of Spring. Book III was the last book written though it was experienced nearly a year beforehand. It was written during sixteen days of April 2015 – a number of

Crowns

The Bride, whose symbolism has already been discussed. But more can be seen through the architecture of the books in the placements of the chapters. As an example, "As A King" falls on the twenty-second chapter of this book, Crowns.

Somewhere between the completion of Gravity Calling and the start of Crowns, my Father began revealing portions of the symbolism that these words – His words – housed. But perhaps the one revelation that means the most to me, is in the way Book VII has a page count that totals 13. Though many may attempt to dismiss numerology, it holds a divine truth for those with eyes to see. In Deuteronomy 6:4, it is written, "Hear, O Israel Hashem our God, Hashem is one." And just as it has been demonstrated in these words how God works in twos, there is a verse in the New Testament that brings truth and guidance to the words from Deuteronomy – a book written over a thousand years before Jesus walked the Earth. In John 4:8 it is written, "He that Loveth not, knoweth not Hashem, for Hashem is Love." The word Hashem is the Hebrew word used for Lord. Modern translations choose to use the word "Lord" or "God" to represent the many names that refer to God throughout the Biblical canon. And while it is obvious that the words intend to illustrate God is Love, the number 13 would not be readily apparent without the two verses seen as One. So through these two verses, it can be seen that:

...

Hashem is Echad (which means "one" in Hebrew).
Echad is Ahavah (Hebrew for Love).
Therefore, Hashem is Ahavah.

A Place For Everything

...

Ahavah is a word created from the Hebrew letters Aleph, Hey, Beyt, Hey. These letters carry the numerical values of 1, 5, 2, 5 – which, when added together equal 13. Though there are other Hebrew words for Love, Ahavah is the only word that can used to represent Love because it must carry the same numerical value as Echad, which equals 13. Though it is understandably a lot to process in understanding the words written, the most important thing to take away is to understand it Is. The words written from the beginning of time were divinely architected to survive generations of divide. And when the time came for the Lord to prepare the world for the Messiah's return, He would do so across divides by revealing the architecture of His Love.

We are all part of a Love story being written, one that must be left behind for generations. Our time in these last days is not to be taken for granted for there is a judgment upcoming to be placed upon each and every one of us. The Love and the Light we leave behind must be nurtured and cherished for others to one day find. So as these words are completed through the Love story penned by His hand, take heed to always maintain the form in which they were written and printed upon the pages. There is a place for everything and a reason for its placement, so that these words may carry through across oceans of generations – an Ark of Letters upon spiritual waters, His Love embodied in the words, His Gravity Calling us Home.

Confetti Falling Down

In the beginning, I was led to include a chapter from The Great Gatsby in Lindsey's edition of Gravity Calling for reasons I could not justify in earthly explanation. I knew it was important to add content of misdirection so she would not initially see the book's ending, but the reasoning and rationale for including a chapter from The Great Gatsby was a mystery to me. After finding a version of the book to use, I realized due to the length of each of the nine chapters included, all I needed was one chapter to fill the ending of Gravity Calling. When I chose chapter seven, it was just a symbolic gesture for the story. But perhaps the final words that were written, were divinely chosen for the journey on which I was being led. The final portion of chapter seven of The Great Gatsby, ends with this closing dialogue – a definition of spiritual Love unending, witnessed through earthly eyes.

...

Trimalchio was waiting where I had left him in the drive.

"Is it all quiet up there?" he asked anxiously.

"Yes, it's all quiet." I hesitated. "You'd better come home and get some sleep."

He shook his head.

"I want to wait here till Daisy goes to bed. Good night, old sport."

Crowns

He put his hands in his coat pockets and turned back eagerly to his scrutiny of the house, as though my presence marred the sacredness of the vigil. So I walked away and left him standing there in the moonlight – watching over nothing.

...

Though it is an often missed interpretation of the story of Gatsby, it should very much be viewed for the spiritual meaning. If nothing else, the number of the chapters should signal a divine notion, and the stories housed within their respective chapters, an even deeper symbolism. Fitzgerald divided the story into nine chapters – each chapter symbolic to the nine spiritual divisions. The seventh chapter – the chapter I was led to include in Lindsey's edition of Gravity Calling – is the portion of the story where Gatsby, who has an unending Love for Daisy, begins to understand what Love is truly about. Chapter Seven could best be understood as Love's spiritual transcendence. All that Gatsby had to offer – a perfect Love and all of the wealth in the world – could not win over the heart of Daisy. He had a Love so grand that he threw party after party in hopes of catching her attention. He kept a green light burning on his dock in hopes she would see him. He committed every ounce of his life to seeking her out while never saying directly, "Here I am." It was a demonstration of Love so grand, interpreted by most as the Love of an empty man.

But for the truth of the story to be revealed, the story should be viewed through the eyes of our Father. For the beautiful craft of Fitzgerald's work is in the way he paints a picture of Gatsby as the empty man, though the spiritual version demonstrates how He has an unending Love within. If it could be seen that Gatsby's life was the embodiment of the Spirit, then the entire story could be re-explored on this premise. This was the very foundation of Fitzgerald's work, though most critics will only see it for the political prose. When it is viewed in the light of Gatsby as the Spirit, it could be seen how a perfect Love of our Father goes unnoticed and is generally unwelcomed unless there is direct benefit. The lights, the symbolism, the jealousy of others – is all indicative of a spiritual Love greater than earthly desire. The Love is grander than most can handle, leaving a trail of manmade disaster as seen through the death of Myrtle in the "valley of ashes" – a reference to Psalms 23 in the Bible. It is a moment when Gatsby recognizes his endless Love for Daisy is met with a hopeless void inside. It is a moment when the nature of man is revealed as a conscious lie.

In the end, Gatsby dies, and no one seems to care. He is killed by a jealous man who blames Gatsby for his wife's death. It is the type of action symbolic to how man exclaims to God over the death of a Loved one, "Why did you do this? It is all your fault!" Man attempts to extinguish Love and remove faith from the equation when it was man that was the maleficence of the reason. In the end of the story, no one truly seems to care for Him. People only wanted what He could give them in the moment while they were caught up in the luster of their own earthly nuances. The ending is symbolic to earthly life and the story of finding Christ. For even the ones who say they are "in Love" with the Lord are often still void, empty, and

Crowns

reckless inside. It is a statement of the story that asks the great question, if our Father died, who would really know and who would care? The only evidence would be the absence of grand gestures that are generally received in selfish nature. Would the Love of our Father be great enough to see, if "the Man behind the curtain," removed Himself completely?

I have never seen an analysis of Gatsby assessed through spiritual eyes, but it is easily viewed from this side of the Divide. Many will say the story cannot be of spiritual nature – an irony since the very story is written about this aspect of human nature. But to those people who seek truth through all facets of light, the name "Trimalchio" mentioned specifically in chapter seven, should cast a greater insight. It was a name and a chapter that my Father led me to include in Gravity Calling for symbolic reasons I was not aware of at the time, though it is the best part of the story when seen in hindsight.

Perhaps the intentional misdirection for Lindsey was divinely placed into Gravity Calling as juxtaposition to my own misdirection to His foreshadowing of the ending to His Story. For the ending to the version of the Love story Lindsey would receive, was the misdirection as seen through the eyes of a King. Though it would not come to my attention until over a year later, the word Trimalchio is rooted in a Greek prefix and Hebrew form. The name means, "king," "thrice king," and "the greatest king." And just how great of a divine twist it was to have the ending of Gravity Calling revealed before it occurred while foreshadowing the rest of the journey, all as seen through the eyes of the Lord?

Confetti Falling Down

On February 7, 2014 – a day that sums to seven – the ending to Gravity Calling was completed. The following morning after my daughter awoke, we talked about the snow outside and how I likened it to confetti. Somewhere in her little creative mind, she had decided confetti was the same thing as Funfetti (a type of white birthday cake with rainbow colors inside). At the time, we had a good laugh when we finally realized she thought I was talking about cake falling from the sky. Not long after, I would sit down to write about the morning spent with her and the completion of the book from the previous night. Though I would not see how the writing that morning would compare to the ending of chapter seven (the ending of Lindsey's Edition), I wrote the following words as how I thought the next portion of the story would begin.

And it did.

I awoke on February 8, 2014, to God's confetti falling down from the sky. It was the first real snow Nashville had received in 2014, and a type of divine response to the preceding week for me. The previous evening I had just wrapped up the final version of Lindsey's edition of Gravity Calling to be sent to the printer. In it, I added the final Gatsby chapters to mask the ending of the book. The very last thing I did was name the chapters. The final chapter I named "Confetti Falling Down." It really has nothing to do with Gatsby, but rather the way I envisioned the ending of the book drawing to a close. It was the final stroke of editing before I would send it off to the

Crowns

printer. So as I awoke on the February 8th, all I could do was smile when I saw the snow falling down. I had never thought of snow as confetti, but in that moment, I knew that it was a grand acknowledgment in divine timing and circumstance. I made a cup of coffee and just stared out the wall of glass windows of my condo.

Cinderella Love

When the journey began and the first book of this series began to take its form, I had every bit of confidence that I foresaw the story's ending being penned by God's hand all along. Though I was caught somewhere in the middle of the story when my eyes were opened, once I was able to see, I believed His story had fallen into view. What I would not understand was how the script that God was penning had so much more to be revealed. Like a great cliffhanger at the end of a book that no one saw coming, I began to realize that His story being told was filled with cliffhanger after cliffhanger until one day I would understand that it was not the cliff that I needed to be holding on to in order not to fall. I had to fall. I had to let go. And in that, realize the fall was the greatest ascent a human could ever know.

A cliffhanger by its very definition is a point of potential – a point that resides closest to the cusp of the unknown. Would resolve through the impending fill the heart with something great or something foreboding? Would the resolve grant peace or perturbation? Would not knowing the resolve be better than having known it all along? Would a sudden surprise be the resolve always expected, a childlike wonder of resolve to the unknown? Or would somehow the idea of an inevitable let-down destroy all hope? But perhaps the greatest question of all is why would a person ever wonder how it will all turn out, when He has already let us know? The story that He is writing is one that is only ever full of wonder and hope. It is a story of fantastic highs and remarkable lessons to be learned through the perceived lows. The pain people experience through any of the perceived lows should only be seen as a child throwing a tantrum of disrespect to the Creator holding him close. Those with eyes to see should never see an island of desolation, for the ending is always one of light. Being bound by earthly desires is what separates the darkness and the light. The Earth is the veil, used as a guide for our souls to find a better understanding of all that is beneath the veil. The veil is hiding His eyes from His children's until His grand reveal. It is like a game of peekaboo on the most magnificent scale.

In the beginning, I thought His story was a story about Love – a Cinderella Love greater than a human has ever known. It was to be the grand denouement of this trip around the sun. As His words began to be shared with me in the grandest of ways I could never have imagined, I thought I knew it all. Even in my humility, the childlike excitement of thinking I understood all that was to be revealed was a naiveté that should forever be written in the stars. I saw Love – an earthly Love – bound by the hand of Our Creator. It was a Love wrapped up in white lace and blue, that in all of my wildest dreams seemed to be the fairytale ending about to come true.

Cinderella Love

Oh, but the irony of all of the actions He led me to take would only be truly revealed in the end of days. For those actions were never about me, nor about fulfilling the destiny in the way that I thought was the arc of His script all along. The actions were never about a Cinderella Love, nor a Love that would ever be bound upon this Earth. Though the story had to seem that way for His truth to be told, the story was always about Him. His Love. His Almighty Love. The story was told in a way for me to understand, so that one day, I could explain through these words, how everything I experienced upon this portion of my journey was a metaphorical understanding of His Almighty Love. It was only ever an extreme-micro understanding of a macro-magnificent Love.

The true storyline being told was held in the actions of the presentation of the box I gave Lindsey and the contents therein – all on the day I went "All In." In the box that I have already described through the elegance and symbolism of its craft, was placed a book – the first book of this series. At the time, I thought Gravity Calling was the complete story being told – the only book that was to be written. The manner in which the book was packaged and delivered also held a special significance to the symbolism of my efforts in which I was led. The story was important, but the ending seemed more so. However, the book Lindsey received did not contain the ending. Rather, her book ended with a cliffhanger. The real ending I had written was divided across two chapters and placed within two sealed envelopes. One chapter was contained within the envelope I held. The other envelope contained the final chapter and was placed in the safety deposit box for Lindsey to bring with her on her journey, where she would eventually meet me standing upon the sands of the shoreline to the great expanse of the rolling oceans upon this little blue marble.

At the time, it was to be a grand entrance to a Cinderella kind of Love – one that she had to only follow His lead. But the irony was that the story written was a symbolic lesson to the story of His Love – a story that one day would be shared with the world for all to see. For the world would receive Gravity Calling in a manner similar to how Lindsey did – in a cliffhanger to all that could be. His story to eventually be told, would transcend through the events to come, with a resolve that would leave the world breathless, and a man humbled upon his knees. These are the days the story of the first book became the ending, the first and the last, the beginning and the end. The chapters that held the resolve to the cliffhanger ending, would only be revealed at the end of Book III, though with a twist of something unexpectedly special for all of the world to see. He held one portion of the ending, while I held the other portion in a sealed envelope to be carried along the journey until He deemed the time had arrived for me to read the next portion that I was to see. All I ever had to do was open the gift packaged especially for me, to read His words, to understand His Love, to follow His instructions on how to break the clay to reveal the key residing within, and then blindly follow His lead.

Cinderella Love

Every moment of this portion of the journey was divine. Every aspect with Lindsey placed as the focal point of the view was masterfully architected by His Divine hand. Could it have worked out? Absolutely. But perhaps it worked out the way it was always intended. For in a cosmic twist of the storyline, like a child who on Christmas thinks he has figured out what is actually contained within the presents all wrapped up and packaged beneath the tree, my Father's gift left me scratching my head when it was opened up… that is until He said, "Son, let me tell you what you are holding and all that it means." It is at this time that a child is left dumbfounded at the naiveté of his ways, but awestruck to the splendor of something greater hidden behind the ego's desires, no matter how innocent and strong that first desire may have seemed. And, in that, was the most unexpected surprise – the potential held within the resolve sought to all that was hidden beneath.

The gift my Father revealed was in the symbolism of the book and the words contained therein. For within the box that He had me package in the most symbolic of ways, was placed the introduction to the real journey – the one I had yet to see. It was a book penned by Him through the experiences He allowed me to see. It would take another year of divine experiences, travels to the heavens, and the most fantastical of conversations with Our Father, His angels, and His messengers for me to see. He had led me on a journey to share His story to others as He was telling an even greater one to me. The story that I was to experience along the way was intended to be seen as I witnessed it, for that is how we, as humans, have to learn to see. The story that He desired me to see, was one that would fall into focus in the hindsight of the view. For it was on that day I went "All In" to Love, blindly following His words, that God said, "Yes, you are, Son. And though you don't know it yet, there is so much more to be said. I can't wait for you to see the story that has been being told all along. I Love you. So hang on. This ride is about to get real. The ride you thought you boarded was just to get you to the door. The ride you will experience, will be so much...so much more."

It was those words that I would only begin to see as the journey neared its end. Twelve hundred and sixty days of experiencing His grand storytelling was truly walking upon the waters when I thought I was walking upon the land. A faith unbridled in commitment to His words revealed the most unexpected surprise. For some, the mind races at exasperating speeds at the mere mention of the potential of His divine. It is a time that hope is placed in the potential and faith is blindly placed upon the leap. It is a time that hanging onto the edge of the cliff becomes too much of a struggle wherein most will try to find their way back from the edge to solid ground in order to view the cliff from the safety of afar. The rush of sensations of not trusting in His intentions is too much for many to handle. Those are the ones that say, "That's great that you did it, but that isn't something I could do. It isn't something I'm strong enough to do, yet." When, in truth, everyone is strong enough and "yet" is simply an excuse for procrastination and delay. We would never be standing upon this Earth if the next step was impossible to achieve. The perception that a demonstration of faith of this magnitude is impossible is just an excuse of a person saying indirectly to God, "I don't trust You completely." The song to that chorus of words is the saddest song sung upon this Earth, but is also the one that is hummed to the loudest tune. He knows. He hears. He sees. He cries. And, He celebrates when victories are found.

Solid ground is the idea that mankind has some form of safety and dominion over a material world. The view from afar is always safer through the eyes of the ego though the view from the edge is the most spectacular – for it is the view through the eyes of the soul. And while many can crowd along the edge and let everyone know where they are standing, the rare are the ones who hear His voice asking to take mere baby steps to follow Him home. Maybe it is just inching a little closer to a place of discomfort. Maybe a person's closeness to the edge causes fear among those who care about them the most, but are watching from afar. Sometimes the desire to calm others' fears pulls us from where we are all meant to be. It is a pendulum-like effect to the pull of His Voice and the pull from those left behind. But when it is viewed only as a child-like fear of the unknown, it should also be seen through the comfort of those who have taken the steps before others. For the rare who have heard the call and demonstrated their trust have all returned with wondrous stories to share. And for those who haven't returned, those are the ones whose stories of their ascensions will forever be known.

For me, the journey led me to an edge. The edge was initially cloaked in darkness and was the edge to the most delicate and fearful part of my being. The safety and comfort that I had found in keeping my feelings for another at bay kept the frame of my stained-glass structure housing my soul absent of light from within. But, His Voice led me home. His Voice led me to Love. He asked me to keep edging closer to Him and as I did I realized His Hands were holding me all along. As the baby steps became more adult-like in form, I eventually found myself running in full stride. The strides gave way to the revelation of a race I had been running since I was born. I would never have thought the destination was ever leading me to a seat upon a throne. At least, that's what I thought, but now I realize I somehow knew the destination all along.

The strides I took upon this clip of the journey became faster and stronger in form. The edge became a distant ledge that I had leapt from long before I had ever known. To others, perhaps, I disappeared beneath the horizon of the ledge from their points of view. For part of the journey is not revealing all that has been seen until it is meant to be revealed to others. Some will return with grand stories. Some will continue to directly ascend. Some – as in how these books came to be – will continue to write along the way. But it is important to understand that the concept of ascension is trusting in the fall. It is leaving the body behind, wherein somehow the directions of up and down are reversed. The fall is an ascension where the phrase "as above, so below" suddenly makes perfect sense. The hands of God that are holding a person stride-for-stride along the journey's ledge are more like the wings upon the backs of angels, where the wings should be seen as the repre-

Cinderella Love

sentation of a soul learning to have an unbridled trust in the Love of God. It is a learning process, just as a bird must learn to use its wings to fly in order to survive, so must we learn to find an unbridled trust in His Love, to see the world through His eyes, and carry a Love for every soul as a mother, a father, a brother, a sister, and a child.

In the beginning, I thought His story was a story about Love – a Cinderella Love greater than a human has ever known. It was to be the grand denouement of this trip around the sun. As His words began to be shared with me in the grandest of ways I could never have imagined, I thought I knew it all. Even in my humility, the childlike excitement of thinking I understood all that was to be revealed was a naiveté that should forever be written in the stars. I saw Love – an earthly Love – bound by the hand of Our Creator. It was a Love wrapped up in white lace and blue, that in all of my wildest dreams seemed to be the fairytale ending about to come true.

And it Was.

Just as a baby crowns upon being birthed into this world, so does the soul crown upon being birthed into the light of Christ. Through man's eyes, it is a crowning achievement – one in which a crown is placed upon the head in recognition with confetti falling down. To our Father, it is as a baby just being born, a prince in the moment, a king to one day become.

...

May His Gravity Calling take you by the Spirit and endlessly waltz with your soul. Glory be to God, the Almighty.

...

www.ingramcontent.com/pod-product-compliance
Lightning Source LLC
Chambersburg PA
CBHW021145080526
44588CB00008B/224